W9-BKO-537

THE BOOK-PEDDLING PARSON

The Rev. Mason Locke Weems

THE BOOK-PEDDLING PARSON

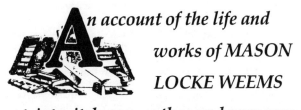

n account of the life and
works of *MASON*
LOCKE WEEMS
patriot, pitchman, author and purveyor
of morality to the citizenry of the early
United States of America.

by **LEWIS LEARY**

Algonquin Books   *1984*

A NOTE ON THE ILLUSTRATIONS

The sketch of Mason Locke Weems appearing opposite the title page is taken from Lawrence C. Wroth, *Parson Weems, a Biographical and Critical Sketch* (1911), where it is identified as "from a print in the possession of D. McN. Stauffer, M. Inst C. E."

Illustrations of Pohick Church, Dumfries, Va.; Belle Air, Dumfries; the handbill in Weems's handwriting; the title pages of the first and ninth editions of Weems's book on George Washington; the siege of Charleston; Sergeant Jasper's rescue of the flag; the title pages and illustrations to *God's Revenge against Drunkenness* and *God's Revenge against Gambling*; and the view of Charleston are from the Rare Book, North Carolina, and general collections of Wilson Library, University of North Carolina at Chapel Hill.

The drawing of Marion's men crossing the Pee Dee River is from the collection of the Florence Museum, Florence, S.C., and is included through the courtesy of Joyce Dowis, curator. The photograph was made by Johnny Ellis of the *Florence Morning News*.

The drawing of the British officer being invited to dine with Francis Marion is in the collection of the Carolina Art Association/Gibbes Art Gallery, Charleston, S.C., and is reproduced through the courtesy of Martha R. Severens, Curator of Collections.

The view of Richmond, Va., 1817, by Peter Maverick, was used as the frontispiece to William Wirt's *Letters of the British Spy*, probably the seventh or eighth edition, and is used by courtesy of the Valentine Museum, Richmond.

The drawing of Washington and the cherry tree appears in *The Life of Washington by Mason L. Weems*, edited by Marcus Cunliffe (Belknap Press of Harvard University Press, 1962).

Hogarth's drawing of the effects of drunkenness is by courtesy of the British Museum, London (Sat. 3136).

© 1984 by Lewis Leary

All rights reserved. Except for brief quotation in critical articles and reviews, this book, or parts thereof, must not be reproduced in any form without permission from the publisher.

ALGONQUIN BOOKS
P.O. Box 2225, Chapel Hill, N.C. 27515–2225

ISBN 0–912697–09–1

LIBRARY OF CONGRESS CATALOGING IN PUBLICATION DATA

Leary, Lewis Gaston, 1906–
    The book-peddling parson.

    Includes index.
    1. Weems, M. L. (Mason Locke), 1759–1825.   2. Authors, American—19th century—Biography.   3. Booksellers and bookselling—United States—Biography.   4. Episcopal Church—United States—Clergy—Biography.   I. Title.
PS3157.w83z75   1984   283'.092'4 [B]   84-341
ISBN 0-912697-09-1

PS
3157
W83
Z15
1984

For Father
who was also a scribbling
and an evangelistic parson

CONTENTS

LIST OF ILLUSTRATIONS

THE BOOK-PEDDLING PARSON

ACKNOWLEDGMENTS

T hroughout the making of this book, I have been unfailingly led by the findings of Emily E. F. Skeel as set forth in the three volumes of her *Mason Locke Weems, His Works and Ways* in which she extended the bibliographical findings of her brother, Worthington C. Ford, and added to them much of the correspondence between Weems and his Philadelphia partner, Mathew Carey. And I have used with great confidence Lawrence C. Wroth's pioneering *Parson Weems: A Biographical and Critical Study*, William Alfred Bryan's sturdy *George Washington in American Literature*, Marcus Cunliffe's fine introduction to his edition of Weems's *Life of Washington* as printed by the Belknap Press of Harvard University Press, James Gilbreath's perceptive monograph on Weems's importance in the history of bookselling in America, "Mason Locke Weems, Mathew Carey and the Southern Book Trade, 1794–1810," in *Publishing History*, X (1981), and, with less assurance, Harold Kellock's sprightly portrayal of *Parson Weems and the Cherry Tree*. To all of them, great thanks.

For help in putting these pages together, thanks go to Paul Koda, curator of Rare Books in the University of North Carolina Library, and to his tireless assistant, Imre Kalanyos; to Robert France of the microfilm dungeon of that library, who contributed to the ruin of my eyesight by teaching me to use tortuous machines in reading card and film reproductions of many of Weems's writings; to Mattie Russell, head of the manuscript collection in the Duke University Library; and to Bambi Grimes who typed indefatigably, to Mary Warren who read with patience, and to my adopted nephew and namesake who turned out to be a merciless but helpful critic of my ways of saying things.

1. INTRODUCTORY

"The Country Is in Darkness"

If the Reverend Mason Locke Weems lives on in American history, it is as the person who supposedly made up the story of young George Washington doing in a cherry tree with his little hatchet, and then refusing to tell a lie about it. He entered that tale into his little book about Washington that in one edition or another has outsold every other book about Washington ever written. Most historians have not forgiven Weems for what he did with the cherry tree and the hatchet. They have written him off as a charlatan and a romancer. But as Parson Weems he endures, a ghost figure on the outskirts of our national literature.

Mason Locke Weems (as far as I can determine, his name was pronounced Wems, as in *gems* or *hems*) was far from a ghost. He was a clergyman and itinerant bookseller who attempted to extend his parish throughout the United States during its formative years, particularly through the American South, by vending books and morality. What he could not find in other people's books to mend the ways and raise the minds of his countrymen, he produced himself. His little paperbacks on the necessity for tolerance, on the dangers of drink, gambling, duelling, and marital infidelity sold widely in many editions, most of them at twenty-five cents each.

He was a democrat complete, devotedly loyal to principles of the new republican government. He took at face value the ringing words of the Declaration of Independence and of his country's new constitution. All men were created equal, with equal rights, but with equal responsibilities also. To help

1

shore up the new republic, he would appeal not only to the wealthy and educated plantation owners or to people trained to lead; he would reach also toward the small farmer with a few acres to tend and a large family to provide for. As a preacher, he would be a teacher also, for schooling had been disrupted in his homeland during the years of struggle for independence. What was needed was education, and he played consistently on that theme. Education depended on the use, in the proper way, of the right kinds of books. He became an evangelist for reading.

"The country is in darkness," he said. At the end of the eighteenth century as his countrymen strove to form a new nation, he found that often people in backcountry areas struggled toward liberty with their thoughts "unformed, their minds bitter, and their manners savage." What could be done about it? "Humanity and Patriotism both cry aloud," he said, "for Books, Books, Books." So, to answer the cry, he travelled from country house to country house, from hamlet to hamlet, from town to town, to fairs, horse races, and public sales, anywhere that people gathered, there to sell books. He preached, he cajoled, some accounts insist that he fiddled saucy tunes to attract people to his book stalls. He was a man with a mission.

Urban centers like Boston, New York, and Philadelphia provided bookstores where a gentleman or a lady might browse among the latest imports from abroad or books of native manufacture. But through much of the South, people who were likely to buy books were scattered, most of them in outlying farms or plantations. Many of their libraries were stocked with fine volumes, many of which had been brought from abroad before the Revolution. They had access to few local publishers of books and few bookstores. Books would somehow have to be brought to them, and to all of them, even to the person cultivating a few acres to provide for a growing family.

2

Such an attempt had been made before. Shortly after the Revolution, Robert Bell, an energetic and effervescent, eccentric Scottish bookseller in Philadelphia, had occasionally shipped a load of books to the South, and had himself followed them, colorfully auctioning them off in public sales. It was as good as a play, people said, to observe his antics and listen to the salty anecdotes that he used to attract people to his sales. But Bell was able to cover only the larger cities of the South, like Charleston and Richmond, and in the latter city he died in the autumn of 1784.

Mathew Carey, an energetic young man, newly arrived in Philadelphia from Ireland, immediately bought up most of Bell's stock and printing equipment, and with them began a long and successful career as one of the new country's most prominent bookmen, but not until ten years later, and then in partnership with Weems, was he to venture into the task of distributing books throughout the South. Theirs became a close but tempestuous relationship extending over thirty years, with one brief interlude when Weems succumbed to the temptation of attempting to get very rich quickly by accepting the sole distributorship throughout the South of Chief Justice John Marshall's multi-volumed official biography of Washington. But, that enterprise proving to be unsatisfactory, he returned chastened to partnership with Carey and died in his service, outdoing even Robert Bell in colorful showmanship.

Weems was more mobile than Bell had been, assiduously travelling to where buyers were to be found, selling books, it has been said, as if they were bottles of snake oil, but convinced that he was performing a service by "disseminating thousands of Excellent Books" among the excellent but often uninformed working people of the South. And he appealed to the wealthy also, offering them the opportunity to subscribe for handsome books with fine embossed covers. He had something for everyone.

His purpose, he said, was "to *Enlighten*, to *dulcify* and *exalt* human nature" by providing books that would preserve the precious freedoms that the young republic had fought so hard to attain, and to enlighten with useful books that pointed ways toward wealth and well-being. As a practical person, he vended practical books, more nonfiction than fiction, and hardly any poetry at all. What fiction he did sell was exemplary fiction, like Goldsmith's *The Vicar of Wakefield* or Susanna Rowson's popular account of the ill-fated, callously seduced *Charlotte Temple*, but mostly in the form of shorter moral tales, many of them by Weems himself, that warned of traps into which the unwary, the uneducated, and the unread might fall.

What is presented here will be found to be less a detailed biography that a presentation of what manner of man Mason Locke Weems was, what he wrote, when he wrote it, and sometimes why. His pamphlets and even most of his longer books have become so rare, so nearly forgotten, that it has seemed proper, and fair to him also, to describe them or quote from them in what may seem excessive, even repetitious detail. Weems was George Washington's biographer, to be sure, and he made into fable the story of young George, his hatchet, and the cherry tree. But he deserves to be remembered for more than that.

He stood, perhaps not always sturdily, at the threshhold of literature in the new United States, particularly that of the American South, discovering in theme and tone much that would later be more artfully presented. As I have read him, I have heard other Southern voices, from Augustus B. Longstreet and Mark Twain to that later outspoken Marylander, H. L. Mencken. I have not always pointed them out, preferring to allow readers their own occasional pleasant shocks of recognition.

It has been pleasant for me to get to know Weems better,

4

and my best hope is that my pleasure can be found to spill over into what I have found to say about him.

His phrasing, his spelling, and his punctuation were those of his time or of his own stalwart idiosyncrasy. I have done nothing, I hope, to spoil their savor.

2. THE MAKING OF A BOOKMAN

"Religion with Irregularity"

nce found guilty of a stretcher, you are forever afterwards a marked person. People are likely to look with suspicion at everything that you say after that.

Just when Mason Locke Weems was first caught stretching truths is not known. Perhaps it was when he identified himself on the title pages of some of his books as having been the Rector of Mount Vernon Parish, when all that he seems to have been was an occasional preacher at a country church near enough to George Washington's home for members of the family, perhaps even the General himself, to have ridden over on a Sunday morning for divine service, perhaps even when Parson Weems was in the pulpit.

Washington, some years before the Revolution, had been a vestryman of Truro Parish where the old Pohick church was located, but had left that parish on taking command of the continental army. The war over, he and most of the gentry of the vicinity worshipped at the more fashionable churches in Annapolis or Alexandria, and it has been suggested that the eighteen miles between Mount Vernon and the struggling old church at Pohick were seldom traversed by him or his family after that.

But perhaps it was earlier than this that Weems was caught out. Some contemporaries even doubted that he had ever been consecrated a clergyman at all. That they have been proved to have been wrong may suggest that some of the stretchers that Weems has been accused of having been guilty of telling were not really stretchers at all, but may be discovered to have been not quite verifiable historical facts, perhaps slightly, but with justifiable good intention, enlarged and enriched in his telling of them. Much of what he may have invented has become legend, securing him a name, if not unsullied fame, as a recorder of the morals and aspirations of his time.

As a man of invention and unadulterated good will, he would not allow the solid angularity of fact to intrude upon an edifying story, any more than he would allow any narrative to be used for other than edifying ends. Truth was an essence, symbolizing something greater than what was said, in the service of which precision could with confidence be sacrificed.

On one thing almost everyone agrees, and that is that Mason Locke Weems was born in St. James Parish, Anne Arundel County, Maryland, on October 11, 1759, the youngest of nineteen children sired by David Weems who early in the century had been brought from Scotland by a bachelor uncle who was said—here tradition takes the place of record—to have been a younger brother of the Earl of Wemyss, and who disappointed his nephew by marrying late in life, thus depriving the younger man of an expected rich inheritance.

But even being described as the nineteenth of his father's children is something of a stretcher, true enough, but misleading. David Weems at eighteen had married in 1724 Elizabeth Lane, who bore him seven children, the third of which was his namesake, David. After her death, he was married again, to Hester (or Esther, sometimes Easter) Hill, a spinster of twenty-five, who during the next seventeen years bore him twelve more, four of them being Davids, appearing in rapid succession between 1747 and 1751, to take the place of the first David, born of his first marriage, who had died the year before the begetting of new Davids began. Of these four Davids, the first three died in infancy, but the fourth lived to become Mason's closest male sibling.

The sons of the first marriage, the oldest of them in his early thirties, the youngest twenty-one, had surely set up households of their own by the time of Mason's birth, so that the family in which he grew up was not inconveniently large, only two brothers and three sisters born of the second marriage surviving at the time of Mason's birth. The prodding influence of their example undoubtedly provided his earliest education. But soon he was off to daily drudgery in schools of St. James Parish, of which his father was a vestryman, and he is said to have been sent briefly for further study with one Daniel Jenefer in Charles County.

Here the first of the legends that have clouded but colored his early life seems to have originated. Often of an evening, it was said, he would disappear from the company of his fellow students, straying away into the woods, perhaps into town with who knows what impious intentions. Suspicious, his friends followed him, only to find their classmate seated in a tumbledown shanty, teaching poor children to write and to read. As retold, in various settings with different people involved—street urchins in London or wide-eyed plantation blacks in the backcountry South—the story does ring with some authenticity, if not in detail of where and when and to whom, at least as testimony to a kind of outgoing altruism that seems to have been characteristic of Mason Weems throughout his life.

After graduation at fourteen, tradition insists "with Honors," from the Kent School at Chestertown, just across the bay from Baltimore, he is said to have set out for Edinburgh for the study of medicine and, that completed, to have sailed at seventeen as a surgeon on a British man-of-war, returning to Maryland only after that colony had joined others on the

North American mainland in rebellion against British rule. His father had died in 1779, and Mason always insisted, in spite of some evidence to the contrary, that he had immediately freed the slaves that came to him then as part of his patrimony.

Here the chronicler must be careful. More stretchers? Perhaps not. He seems to have taken slavery pretty much for granted. And was he really a physician? His writings, early and late, are sprinkled with what seem to be more than a layman's advice on how to remain healthy and therefore useful, and wealthy and wise. Some of his obituaries were to speak of him both as clergyman and physician. He never seems to have pressed that point.

At this time, or perhaps earlier, he is said to have sailed, as a deck hand perhaps, or a supercargo, on vessels belonging to his older brothers, recalling in later years having paddled about on the Mediterranean in a large inverted tortoise shell. Like any person reared near the waters of the Chesapeake Bay, he was familiar with nautical terms, and he sprinkled them through his later writings with unstudied ease.

If young Mason, in his teens, took any part in the revolt of the American colonies, it may have been on board a brother's vessel, perhaps running blockades with supplies for his beleaguered countrymen. Maryland sat quietly in the backwash of much of that war, and the Weems family with it, watching with interest what was happening all around them, to the north, the west, and the south. At least one of his brothers is recorded as having sailed under a letter of marque, but few public records remain, and fewer family accounts.

The war over, young Mason crossed the Atlantic again, to Edinburgh and London also, this time for studies that would lead toward ordination as a clergyman. But no bishop would consecrate a former colonial unless he would swear, as all good Anglican churchmen must, allegiance to the crown. That, to a recently emancipated young American, was manifestly impossible. So Weems sought assistance from John Adams, then at The Hague arranging a treaty of peace, but all the help that countryman could give was to suggest that the young man try for ordination among the Presbyterians of Holland or the Lutherans of Sweden, or, that failing, to wait with patience, hoping that the Parliament might relent.

Meanwhile, he suggested that Weems write to Benjamin Franklin in London, which he did, receiving from that busy statesman less assistance than sympathetic prediction that "a hundred years hence, when people are more enlightened, it would be wonder'd that men of America qualified by learning and piety to pray for and instruct their neighbors should not be permitted so to do till they have made a voyage of eight hundred miles . . . to ask leave of a cross old gentleman at Canterbury who seems to have . . . little regard for the souls of the people of Maryland."

Through his own persistence, perhaps because of the intervention of friends or the common sense of the Parliament, Weems was finally on September 5, 1784, ordained as a deacon by the Bishop of Chester, and a week later was consecrated a priest by the Archbishop of Canterbury, after which he returned, at twenty-four, to become Rector of All Hallows Parish, at South River, Herring Creek, in his native Anne Arundel County. There he officiated until 1789, faithful in attendance at the annual conventions of the Protestant Episcopal Church in Maryland and, though unmarried, active in the formation of the Corporation for the Relief of Widows and Children of Clergyman of that church. He served during most of these years on the Superintending Committee for Church Affairs on the Western Shore, which, no bishop having yet been appointed, was charged with examining candidates for the ministry on their adherence to the doctrine, discipline, and forms of worship of the established church.

The young clergyman seems to have been an outgoing person, ready to mix with and please people of whatever persuasion. Before he had been two years in office, he was invited to join the South River Club, which met monthly for evenings of oyster suppers and good talk. When it came his turn to propose a subject for discussion among its members, he chose as appropriate the question of whether "the use of spiritous liquors, except for cure of ill health" was not "an idle and unnecessary practice?"—certainly a subject on which he as physician (if he were a physician) was qualified to expand.

Hardly more than a year later, he found it necessary to resign his membership in the club, perhaps feeling the pinch of its annual dues of three shillings nine pence a year, perhaps wondering how convivial a clergyman can afford to be, especially one who kept, as he is said to have kept, a school for the young ladies of his parish. But he had an easy way with people, and seems to have made friends as he travelled among them on business of the church.

For he was a clubbable person, capable, said one friend, "of assuming the complexion and entering into the spirit of whatever company" he happened into, an adaptability thought by some to be "inconsistent with the simplicity and circumspection" of a man of the cloth. In conversation with friends, he was even said "to have suggested that a person might play at cards without jeopardizing his reputation as a Christian."

As a churchman, he seems to have been more evangelical than some would have wished him to be, even publicly admitting tolerance toward Methodists. Thomas John Claggart, his associate in affairs of the church throughout the State, who was later to become Maryland's first Protestant Episcopal bishop, thought it improper that an ordained priest of that church should publicly admit that followers of John Wesley might have as much hope for salvation as members of the rightfully established church. "I have regard for Mr. Weems," he said. "His zeal and attention to the duties of his sacred office merit esteem, but in proportion as his zeal and

11

diligence are applied to the Methodist interest, it weakens us."

Weems seems to have been informal in the pulpit, addicted to long rhetorical flights, more emotional than logical, appealing to the heart rather than to the head. Even a friend who wished him well admitted himself to be "by no means pleased with that method of working up the passions that pays no respect to reason or decency. A certain pitch of voice or rather vociferation with but now and then a distinguishable word of correspondent horror raised the storm rather by sympathy than by rational concern." But, his friend continued, "whether there be more smoak or fire, I am persuaded that Christ is glorified and therefore rejoice and will rejoice. Religion with irregularity," he thought, "is better than no religion." He found it curious that Weems even attempted to instruct blacks on their right to redemption, "a charitable attempt," he thought. "I hope it will be successful."

But success of all kinds did not come to the rector of All Hallows. The little church, which in colonial times had been supported by levies on each family in the parish, now limped along with only the voluntary contributions from its congregation, apparently barely supplying a living even to a bachelor priest. By the end of 1789, Weems found it necessary to leave.

It has been said, but not attested, that the vestry of Christ Church in Annapolis, of which George Washington at that time was a communicant, voted in 1790 to authorize its rector "to employ as an assistant the Rev. Mason L. Weems, or any other man he should choose," but no record is found of anything coming of that. Instead he accepted appointment as rector of St. Margarets in Westminster Parish. He travelled again as a member of the Superintending Committee for the Western Shore, and undoubtedly served his congregation well.

Those who liked him found him to be "remarkable for his

zeal and industry," but he seems not to have been popular among all of his fellow clergymen or even among some of the people to whom he preached. A colleague spoke of "the dislike and disapprobation he meets with," which might be attributable, he thought "to that diabolical spirit which is enmity against God." He admitted that Weems, though zealous, could sometimes be "tedious in exhortation."

In all, he seems to have been, if not a failed, then an unsatisfactory parson, unsuited to the rigorous and repetitious demands of a country parish or the approval of colleagues who misinterpreted his hortatory zeal. At thirty-two he looked for larger opportunities.

What could be more appropriate for a clergyman than to attempt to spread the gospel through the circulation of sound books that explained religion and right living? So, while still rector of Westminster, Weems had a printer in Wilmington, Delaware, bring out a volume of sermons by the eminent British divine Robert Russell, especially "printed for M. L. Weems." Books from abroad could be had for the taking. No copyright protected them. And a vigorous young man might extend his parish by travelling through the countryside supplementing his income by seeing to it that as many as possible were sold.

Soon he enlisted clerical colleagues in circulating subscription papers through Maryland and Virginia for an ambitious two-volume edition of the sermons of Hugh Blair of Edinburgh, sermons which he said, were unquestionably "the most rational and elegant of their kind." Every household should have these "handsome volumes, printed with a new type on the best paper, neatly bound, lettered and filletted," all for two dollars, and with each subscriber's name prominently printed in each volume.

But sermons sold slowly. Better suited to the taste of many readers was Hannah More's more loosely written and sentimental *An Estimate of the Religion of the Fashionable World,* "the first American edition" of which was "printed and sold by the Rev. M. L. Weems," this and little chapbooks like *Twelve Cents Worth of Wit, or Little Stories for Little Folk of All Denominations*.

Churchless for several years after 1791, Weems roamed the countryside, plodding on foot, on horseback, or in sulky or chaise from one neighboring settlement or plantation house to another, selling some books, seeking subscriptions to others that he would supply, saddening some of his clerical colleagues by his "peddling way of life."

Edifying books did best, but Weems came a cropper with *Onania*, a small treatise on "the heinous sin of self-pollution and all its frightful consequences in both sexes," offering "spiritual and physical advice" on how it might be overcome." He "incurred," said one friend, "a good deal of ridicule as well as serious blame" because of his distribution of this "odd publication." Though it sold well, and "was seen in a good many hands," its popularity was thought to be "rather as a matter of diversion than serious consideration." Whether read to shreds or destroyed in outrage, no copy seems to have survived.

Soon Weems became, not only a seller, but a maker of books, starting in a small way with an abridgment of George Keate's *Account of the Pelew Islands*, choosing for reprint into a small and saleable volume those parts which underlined the brave adventures of seamen marooned on a South Sea island. He was learning that small books sold better than large books, that sometimes even a single chapter might be lifted from a book to become a very sellable item, especially if it told of adventures, most especially if it edified. Even among the best of writers, "verbosities and garrulities will creep in," he said, "to frighten timid readers."

He took first steps toward authorship, and producing his first instant best seller, by editing and expanding the fifteenth-century Venetian nobleman Luigi Cornaro's *Sure and*

Certain Methods of Attaining a Long and Healthy Life, advertised during the late spring and summer of 1793 in newspapers in Maryland, Delaware, and Pennsylvania as a bargain indeed: "The London edition . . . sold at 6/6," while "the American edition, on good paper and filletted with gold," would sell "for 3/3 only."

As an appendix to Cornaro's admonitions on temperance, Weems put together a list of the "Golden Rules of Health" as set forth by Hippocrates, Plutarch, and "several other learned physicians and philosophers" which he introduced and commented on with admonitions of his own. "Of all the people on the face of the earth," he said, "Americans are under the greatest obligations to live temperately." He must have been thinking of his own Maryland lowlands when he explained that "our country abounds in bays, rivers, and creeks, the exhalations of which give the air a dampness unfriendly to the springs of life. To counteract this infelicity of climate, reason teaches us," he said, "to adopt every measure that may give tone and vigor to the constitution."

He spoke as a man of sense, but perhaps as a physician also when he explained that special precautions must be taken in the fall of the year, "for then the body is relaxed by the intense heat of the dog-days," and the air is "filled with noxious vapors from decaying vegetables." Then "Nature herself wears a sickly, drooping aspect; the most robust feel a disagreeable weariness and soreness of their flesh, a heaviness and sluggishness in motion, quick feverish flushings, and sudden chills darting along their nerves. Now, if ever, we need the aid of all-invigorating temperance, now keep the stomach light and vigorous by moderate feeding, the veins well stored with healthy blood, and the nerves well braced by manly exercise and comely chearfulness."

Diet especially must be carefully controlled—only "fruits perfectly ripe, vegetables thoroughly done, and meats of the easiest digestion, with a glass or two of generous wine at each meal, and all taken in such prudent moderation as not to load but strengthen the constitution." For in these dangerous days of autumn, "a single act of intemperance, which would scarcely be felt in the wholesome frosts of winter, often turns the scales against nature and brings an obstinate indigestion . . . a furred tongue, yellowness of eyes, bitter taste in mouth in the morning, bilious vomitings, agues, fevers."

But winter also had its perils. Quoting Thomas Syndenham on "the giddy practice of throwing aside our winter clothes too early in the spring" or "of exposing our bodies, when overheated, to sudden cold," Dr. Weems attests that "many a charming girl, worthy of a tender husband, has sunk into the icy embraces of death, by suddenly exposing her delicate frame, warm from the ball-room, to the cold air."

And then the Rev. Mr. Weems adds his testimony that "many a good soul, with more piety than prudence, turning out quite warm from a crowded preaching into the cold air without a cloak or surtout, has gone off in a galloping consumption to that happy world where pain and sickness are unknown." What a melancholy thing it is, interrupts the physician, Dr. Weems, "that people cannot take care of their souls without neglecting their bodies, nor seek salvation without ruining their health."

Following a statement attributed to Plutarch about the danger of talking so loudly that the blood vessels of the lungs burst, the clergyman speaks again: "Would to God, all ministers of religion . . . would but attend to the advice of this eminent Philosopher. They would, many of them, live longer, and consequently stand a good chance to be more useful here on earth, and brighter saints in heaven. What can give greater pain to a man who has the prosperity of religion at heart, than to see a amiable, pious young man, who promised great services to the world, spitting up his lungs, and dying of a consumption brought on by preaching ten times louder than he had need." Perhaps he remembered his own pulpit style when he said, "Since the world began, no man ever spoke with half the energy which the interest of eternal souls deserve, but there is a wide difference between a moving, melting eloquence, and a loud, unmeaning monotony."

Of all destroyers of health, gluttony was the chief. Physician and clergyman join in quoting both Hippocrates and Ecclesiastes in recommending that a person who has eaten too much should immediately "go forth and puke." But it is the physician who interjects a warning about the "very ruinous error into which too many are fond of running, I mean the frequent use of strong vomits and purgatives." The only medicine that can cure gluttony he insists, is "moderate exercise, innocent amusement, and a little abstinence." And no one should suddenly go from high living to temperance without first consulting a reliable physician.

Gluttony seems to have been a subject on which Weems had strong feelings. People simply ate too much, and then to cure themselves ate even more, tempting outraged stomachs with "drams, slings, elixir of vitriol, wines and bitters, pickles and sauces," entirely disordering themselves until they are overcome with a "general heaviness and weariness of body, flatulent uneasiness, frequent eructations," together with "disturbed slumber" and "frightful dreams," and then "immediately take a dose of tartar emetic or a strong purgative, to cleanse out the stomach and prepare for another course of high living." How dismal an existence, and how contrary to nature and good sense.

People are best served by observing the order of the universe. Daylight is intended for activity, nighttime for rest: "nothing is more injurious to the health than hard study at night; it is inverting the order of nature" and is ruinous of the constitution. "But most of all," he insisted, "it is improper to lie reading in bed." That "not only partakes of the usual inconveniencies of night study, such as straining the eyes, weakening the sight, fatiguing the mind and wearing away

17

the constitution, but is often times the cause of saddest calamities" when candles ignite bedclothes or draperies: "thousands of elegant houses with all their costly furniture have been reduced to ashes by this very imprudent practice."

As the twig is bent, so grows the tree. By spoiling their children, parents will inevitably taste "the bitter waters of their undutifulness or wickedness. Why should we wonder that he who has been accustomed to every thing when in coats, should desire and contend for it in breeches? Youth is the golden season to inure the mind to the practice of virtue" on "which their future health and prosperity depend." Vice is utterly inconsistent with health, which "can never dwell with lewdness, luxury, sloth and violent passions."

For the "life of the epicure and rake is not only short, but miserable," leading to "a gloomy dispirited, dying life," tedious to those who lead it "and troublesome to all around them; and (which is still more pitiable) is often passed on to their innocent unhappy offspring."

With these instructive words, the corrective voice of Mason Weems was first heard over the land. Cornaro's little tract on temperate living and Weems's appended remarks which applied them to life in America was reprinted again and again during his lifetime, sometimes shored up by adding to it Benjamin Franklin's "Way to Wealth" or "Advice to a Young Tradesman" or some other brief admonition about health and happiness.

Renamed in most subsequent editions *The Immortal Mentor*, it became for more than twenty years, if not a consistent best seller, a consistent reminder that Weems had not only the best interests of his readers in mind, but had discovered by 1793 a sprightly admonitory tone to which readers responded. If only the printer would supply him with enough copies, he thought that in six months he might even make a thousand dollars of "clear profit."

When three years later he ventured a second edition under

its new title, he sent a copy to George Washington, who acknowledged the gift by writing, "I have perused it with great satisfaction, and hesitate not to say that it is, in my opinion at least an invaluable compilation. I cannot but hope that a book whose contents do such credit to its title, will meet a very generous patronage. Should that patronage equal my wishes, you will have no reason to regret that you printed the Immortal Mentor."

Weems immediately had the letter printed and pasted into each remaining copy of the book, and in subsequent editions had it printed as an introduction to the text. He was certain that now he could certainly sell "Immense numbers," and he apparently did, grumbling that the printer failed to send him copies enough to meet the demand.

The Washington connection had begun.

3. THE PEDDLING WAY OF LIFE

"Much Joy, Honor, Profit"

y that time, possibly as a result of his having visited Philadelphia to see to the printing there of another saleable book, Weems had met and entered into a business arrangement with Mathew Carey which by the end of 1794 considerably altered and expanded his method of living and of selling books.

Carey was a young Irishman who had come to Philadelphia in the early 1780s, setting himself up there as a printer and publisher. Industrious and alert, with his eye on the main chance, he was soon to become among the most successful of his fellows in the making and distribution of books. And Weems, just a little older than he, became an important instrument in that success. May we, he piously expostulated, only print or reprint "such books as may do good in society."

"This country," he wrote, speaking of Virginia, "is large, and numerous are its inhabitants; to cultivate among them a taste for reading . . . were at once the work of a true philanthropist and prudent speculator. For I am verily assured," he told Carey, "that under the proper culture every dollar that you shall scatter on the field of this experiment will yield you thirty, sixty and one hundred fold." And provide profit for Weems also.

For more careful attention to profit now became necessary.

At thirty-five, the itinerate bachelor salesman was married, on July 2, 1795, to Frances Ewell, the twenty-year-old daughter of a prominent tidewater Virginia family. Her father, Col. Jesse Ewell, was a merchant of Dumfries, then a flourishing town and a center for the exporting of tobacco.

There Weems was to make his home, when he was at home, first in a house in town "with a capital room for the display of books," and then, on the death of Mrs. Weems's father, at Belle Air, the Ewell plantation house some miles north of the town. He took over the care of the old Pohick Parish, and preached occasionally in neighboring churches. During the next seventeen years he sired ten children, only four of whom were to survive him.

Increasing cares meant increasing travel, "beating up the headquarters," Weems said, "of all the old planters and farmers" of Maryland, Virginia, and North Carolina, and even venturing into the "dutchified" society near Lancaster in western Pennsylvania. "A stoney turnpike," he admitted, "seems to promise but a hessian fly sort of harvest," but "by paying all dues to the ancient injunction, I mean by being instant in season and out of season . . . travelling, vending, and collecting," displaying his wares at crossroad stores, isolated mills, country houses, and among relatives and friends, being sure not to miss county court days or fair days when people gathered for sport, frolicking, a little politicking, some exchange of news and gossip, and, Weems hoped, some considerable buying of edifying books.

Though much of his business was in selling subscriptions for books, some of which Carey would print only when he was satisfied that they would be profitable, Weems had also a stock of books on hand, saleable books of all kinds—romances, plays, religious tracts, whatever Carey could provide or that he, with an ear quick to respond to discovery of what people liked, could get printed himself. Even the works of

SAINT PETER'S COLLEGE LIBRARY
JERSEY CITY, NEW JERSEY 07306

that patriot turned infidel, Thomas Paine, were offered for sale, cut down and carefully edited, to be sure, for certainly, thought Weems, some parts of *The Age of Reason* should be kept out of the hands of young readers.

On one occasion, on a court day in Fairfax County, when he was publicly extolling Paine's volume, a disapproving clerical colleague is said to have asked him, "Is it possible that you can sell such a book?" Of course it is, answered Weems, but I also sell the Bishop of Llandaff's reply to Paine. "Behold the antidote," he said, as he picked from his stock of books the bishop's reasoned remarks. "The bane and the antidote are both before you." Truth will win out.

People had a right to read, and he had a responsibility to encourage them to read the right books. A living might thus be made at doing good. As he travelled through the countryside, fine people could be met. He was especially taken by St. George Tucker of Williamsburg, and he suggested that Carey might find it profitable to bid quickly for the publication rights to Tucker's proposed Americanized version of Blackstone on law. But Carey demurred. The project was too expensive.

Expenses also troubled Weems. He did not mind travelling, but the money spent in getting from one place to another bothered him. In one trip, and that only to Richmond, five dollars were spent for coach fare in getting there, five more dollars for getting back to Dumfries, and five dollars beyond that for food and lodging for three days and three nights, that not including "drams for drivers, half bits for Negro waiters," and other "petty larceny robberies to which flesh and blood on the highways is heir to." Mark Twain himself could not have expressed himself more explosively.

It was not easy, this "rolling and jolting, tumbling and tossing thro a journey of 200 miles, rous'd from sweet sleep at one o'clock in the morning, copp'd up in a common stage for almost three days and nights together, my head aching for loss of rest, my ears startled with female screams and masculine imprecations," and "senses stun'd with rattling wheels, crackling whips, and clouds of dust."

He was later to have a wagon of his own, outfitted, it is said, with bookshelves and waterproofed storage cases, even with a hammock strung across from one sturdy upright to another, and with a boy to drive for him. But for now he trudged or drove or rode by stage, picking up at port or postal stop cases of books sent to him by Carey, or driving his chaise from one local printer to another to have books of his own choosing prepared for sale.

Both an adroit salesman and a canny sales manager, he explained to Carey, "Whenever I enter a town, I sell all that I can to subscribers on the spot, and leave the rest in the hands of adjutants, good men and true to sell and hold the money 'till I return." He enlisted friends, relatives (one good aunt of his would have her coachman, he said, deliver whatever books she sold), former schoolmates, clergymen, and physicians in a network of sales people to help him spread culture and to share with him in the profit. He was particularly proud that Judge James Madison of Williamsburg would see to the distribution of books there.

There was much to worry about, to watch over. Books sent by stage or packet from Philadelphia were sometimes carelessly packed, their contents gouged by nails or soiled by water. Weems wished that he might teach those northern people how properly to package books. On that, at least, he said, he was an expert. And sometimes a set would arrive, one volume stamped on the cover with one pattern, another volume with another. Little things like that were important. He reminded Carey that Virginians were fond of pretty bindings, but of pretty bindings that matched.

Above all, he asked that one copy of a book not be sent to

him printed on thin paper, when another copy was printed on heavy paper. The person to whom a thin paper volume was delivered invariably thought that his neighbor with a volume on thicker paper had the better book. Murmurs of discontent rose among his customers, "many of whom are vociferous against me for giving their neighbors the handsomest books." Some of his best customers were cultivated Virginia gentlemen who knew and appreciated the best. He wanted no city tricks played on them.

But he knew some tricks himself. Though filled with enthusiasm, he knew when to be cautious. Not even the United States postal service was to be trusted. When you send me money, he advised Carey, be sure to cut each bill diagonally in half, sending one half to me in one mailing, the other half in another. He had to be adroit in changing Virginia currency to Pennsylvania currency, and Pennsylvanian to Virginian. There was opportunity for making small profits with each exchange. That attracted a person as ingenious as Weems.

Sometimes Mathew Carey had to pull him up short, lest his partner's newly discovered financial expertise undo them both. Remember, he cautioned, the story of the goose that laid the golden eggs. Selling is the goose. Profits the eggs, but avarice is the butcher that wants all the eggs at once. With care, he said, "I feel perfectly satisfied that you can realize two thousand dollars a year and retain the goose in good and improving condition."

Snug in Philadelphia, what did Carey know of the trials and vexations of a salesman on the road? Oh, wrote Weems, "if you could but know the globules of rich sweat, the tears of grief I have shed in consequence of your ill treatment of me, your oppressing and crushing me to earth" by unloading on me books that cannot possibly be sold, books that would not sell in Pennsylvania and were now to be passed on to innocents in the South. That would not do. "If you but knew," he told Carey, "the long and melancholy and expensive journeys I have made with these books, dragging them into every hole and corner of the State." Please stop sending me grim books that cannot be sold anywhere.

Send me cheerful books "of the gay and sprightly kind, novels, decent plays, elegant histories. Let the moral and religious be as dulcified as possible. Divinity for this climate," by which he meant Virginia and Maryland, "should be natural and liberal, adorned with the graces of style, and clothed in splendid binding." As for North Carolina, "great numbers of little entertaining books may be sold there."

Or anywhere else. Weems's experience increasingly convinced him that little books sold better than big books. Big books brought larger profits, volume by volume. But little books sold faster—soft-covered, paperback books that fit easily in purse or pocket. For twelve cents, even twenty-five, a lot of good reading could be spread about the countryside, edifying but exciting, and profitable also. "There is an infinite demand," he discovered, "among store-keepers for spelling books," which brought in not much profit, book by book, but sold in bulk could fill a seller's purse.

These, and voyages, novels, little histories, tales of adventure and decent romance, did well, much better than some of the pious religious tracts that Carey insisted on sending: "you might as well send fiddles to a Methodist conventicle."

But, he assured his partner, "as neither of us are old yet, and may, if you play your cards right, do a great deal together . . . it becomes our mutual wish to print none but such books as may afford a sincere and lasting satisfaction to our Patrons." We must "know that it is not enough for either of us, that Gentlemen impelld by curiosity and high expectation, readily subscribe and honourably pay for our books, we wd above all things, that they shd, after perusal, pronounce them Masterpieces of the Utile & Dulce, and ever regard us as men of Taste and Honour. . . . 'Tis in your power to do great things in this country, if you will but follow my prescriptions."

Weems brimmed over with projects. How profitable it could be, he said, if Carey would put together at regular intervals, perhaps once each month, a collection of popular small books, carefully selected and carefully crated, to be sent to carefully selected agents throughout his territory. Or better, might not a chain of bookstores be set up and kept stocked by regular shipments of books provided by Carey, with Weems on hand to inspect, supervise, and collect profits from each store? "Great prudence," he said, would of course have to be exercised "in choosing the proper men" to manage the stores and in "accomadating books to neighborhoods," and there would have to be "great industry," also, if the project were to succeed.

This he could supply in plenty. Though cares increased, Weems's energy seemed boundless. He speaks of the mounting of parochial duties and of struggling to raise money for his parish at Dumfries. His increasing family brought increasing cares. His horse died, and had to be replaced, and expensively. Carriages broke down because of continuous poundings over rutted roads. Exposure to winter weather brought on chills and fevers. The heat of summer brought fatigue. But nothing seemed to dull his spirits.

He talked of a lottery to help in the establishment of charity schools throughout Virginia: "To all good Christians the cause of the poor and fatherless is," he said, "a primary wish." He was sure that George Washington would be glad to lend his name to such an endeavor: "Philanthropy, Glory, Interest, every thing says that it must and will succeed." The "more we educate the young" and "enlighten the public mind," he reminded Carey, the more we will "bring much joy, honor" and, not least, "profit to ourselves."

Literature must be democratized. Its appeal must not be only to the wealthy and the educated. It must reach all people, and at prices that they can afford. "Experience has taught me," said Weems, that "quarter of a dollar books, on subjects calculated to strike the popular curiosity, printed in large numbers and properly distributed," can provide "an immense revenue to the prudent and industrious Undertaker." He urged Carey to see to the preparation of a series of brief lives of heroes of the American Revolution, men like Generals Wayne, Putnam, and Green, "men whose patriotism and valor" could be held forth as examples. He even suggested that he might write one himself.

Meanwhile, in the early spring of 1799 he wrote and published the first in a series of small books that established him as an author complete and provided examples of the kinds of writing that he had guaranteed, and now proved, would sell and sell well. He called it *The Philanthropist; or a Good Twelve Cents Worth of Political Love Powder for the Fair Daughters and Patriotic Sons of Virginia.* Its price was later raised to twenty-five cents, but even at that it sold well over many years.

It was dedicated to George Washington, with the hope, said its author, "that you may live to see us all, your loving countrymen, catching from your fair example, that reverence for the Eternal Being; that veneration for the laws, that infinite concern for National Union; that inextinguishable love for our country; and that insuperable contempt of pleasures, of dangers, and of death itself, in its services, which have raised you to immortality, and which alone can exalt us to be a great and happy republic."

The dedication was signed by "Your very sincere friend, and Masonic brother, M. L. Weems," who then proceeds through thirty pages to define equality and to plead for less bickering between Federalists and Republicans. In later editions its subtitle became "Political Love Powder for Honest Adamites and Jeffersonians" or "Political Peace-Maker between Honest Men of All Parties."

Washington responded to Weems's dedicatory praise in a letter that was prominently printed in all subsequent editions and in advertisements for them that appeared in newspapers as far south as Charleston. "Much indeed it is to be wished," Washington wrote, "that all the sentiments contained in the Pamphlet and the doctrines it endeavors to inculcate, were more prevalent. Happy would it be for this country at least, if they were so. But while the passions of Mankind are under so little restraint as they are among us, and while there are so many motives, and views, to bring them into action we may wish for but never see the accomplishment of it."

Weems was more optimistic, as well he might be. *The Philanthropist* became popular immediately, going through at least ten editions during the next decade. Four thousand copies of the first edition were printed—"I shall make," Weems said, "large profit." Three days after it first appeared, he boasted to Carey that he had already "sold 350 at a dollar a dozen."

Again, as he had in his edition of Cornaro's book on temperance, Weems both condensed and enlarged another person's work. This time, it was the *Essay on the Natural Equality of Man* by the Rev. William Lawrence Brown of Aberdeen, which had appeared some years before in England and, unprotected by copyright, had been reprinted in Philadelphia. In thus making a little book out of another person's bigger book, Weems lifted with no apparent twinge of conscience sentences and even paragraphs, livening them with what he called "curious anecdotes" of his own. Weems was "ingenious," it has been said, "in dove-tailing, in cutting, clipping, fitting, contriving and furbishing. . . . He could alternate between pen, paste, and scissors with rare felicity."

And with dramatic flourishes also. What, all men created equal? "Soho! what plague have we got now? . . . All man equal! All men equal!!! What my overseer equal to me! Here's a pretty love powder for us truly. An arrant dose of Jacobism I'll warrant it, sufficient to poison a nation."

A reaction like that, said Weems, "is just what I apprehended; for some gentlemen the moment they hear the mention of equality, fancy they see a host of hungry sans-culottes in full march toward desolution, equalling all property, levelling all distinctions, knocking down kings, clapping up beggars and waving the tri-coloured flag of anarchy, confusion and wretchedness, over the ruins of happiness and order." From equality such as this, he continued, "good Lord deliver us" The equality of which he spoke was "an equality of mutual dependence, of civil obligation, of social affection, of dutiful obedience to the laws, and of harmonious co-exertion to make ourselves and our country happy."

People do differ, and that is as it should be. The great body politic is like the human body. It has head, arms, feet, and stomach also. Each part is endowed with a function of its own. In a society, all cannot lead. Some must follow. Some are "made to direct; others to obey." That is democratic equality, and that is what the true philanthropist requires. Weems used native examples to prove that point.

Of course, he explained, some people are larger than others. Some are dwarfs of pigmy size. Others, like the massive legendary Peter Francisco of Virginia, "possess a degree of bodily strength that is truly astonishing." Francisco "has been known to lift a cannon of 1500 weight, and to throw a stout bully over the pales of a garden with great ease. He was at the famous battle of Eutaw Springs," where "he had lead the host of Columbia," and "with no better weapon than a cutlass . . . got a blow apiece at four grenadiers," each blow being "ready money for old Charon."

And some men plod slowly, their eyes on the ground and their hands on the plow. Others walk steadfastly on errands of good will. Still others "swift-footed as the roebuck can bound across fields with the motion of the winds," as did "Col. Daniel Boone, the father of Kentucky, who in his flight from the Indians, ran upwards of one hundred and fifty miles," said Weems, "in twenty-four hours."

Solid American examples pile one on the other. Some people are brighter than others, like the astronomer David Rittenhouse of Philadelphia, of whom Thomas Jefferson is quoted as having said that, "though he never made a world, he came nearer to it than any man ever did," or like Benjamin Franklin, who, though brought up only as "a poor Printer's boy, soon learnt the art to chain the thunderbolts of heaven, and to bid fierce lightnings play harmlessly about our buildings." Nor was Virginia's Patrick Henry to be forgotten, he who "can lead the passions of men about with as much ease as his countryman calls his pigs after him."

But consider the poor Indian. "With a flint tomahawk he hacks down a dozen or two of saplings; these he sets upon end, ties the top, and covers with bark and mud, leaving a hole just big enough for himself and his dog to creep in and out at. This is his wigwam, his castle, his palace. In the midst of this he kindles a fire, around which he yawns and dozes away his gloomy winters. With no cloaths but skins torn from the quivering limbs of Wolfs and Bears, no food but acorns and carcasses of such animals as he has mastered with his club and bow; no music but hissing serpents, screaming wild cats, or the storm howling through the forest."

The Indian was on America's conscience. At just this time Philip Freneau was writing of the Indian as a people with strange but praiseworthy burial habits and good intentions about educating themselves, Charles Brockden Brown was introducing the Indian, his wiles and ways, into native fiction, and John Lathrop, Jr., was preparing a long apologia in verse about what white people had done to red people. To Weems, as to these others, there were few really noble savages among the American aborigines.

The Indian represented man in isolation, alone in the wilderness with no social ties to sustain him. "Thus destitute in his condition, thus imperfect the happiness of the man who has none to help him. . . . His body embraces a number of senses, such as seeing, hearing, tasting, &c. which are so many pleasant inlets to a vaste variety of gratifications; and to this mind, with its capacities, for all the far sublimer pleasures of knowledge, virtue, beauty, painting, poetry, harmony"—these things that nature alone cannot supply, the Indian lacks.

Americans may be grateful not to live, as the Indian must, in isolation. One body, made of many parts, each sustaining the other, Americans "come together for mutual safety and benefit. . . . Convinced of their extreme feebleness while alone, they come together for mutual strength. And so it is with man: the head needs the arms for dexterity, the legs for mobility; each is an equal part of the whole." And so it is, has been, and ever must be in a properly organized society.

The man of thought needs the man of action, and the man of action depends for direction on the man of thought. The scientist, the artisan, the farmer, the explorer are each equal parts of the whole: "the old counsel the young, the wise teach the ignorant, the bold encourage the timid." That is equality: "Alone each man is but a poor shipwrecked sailor caste on a desolate island, where he is hard put to it for berries and roots to keep him from starving. But . . . in our associated state we are like a great family of brothers whom God . . . has endowed with suitable talents, giving this to one, that to another, so that we can now most easily command all conveniences and elegances of a happy life."

Come, fellow citizens of our great republic, he commands. "All hands to quarters—fore and aft a clean ship—up hammocks—light the matches, and stand by to make up thunder— now many hearts be stout and bold. The flag of Columbia waves over their heads, the heroes eye the beloved stripes.

The smile of joy is on their countenances, and the fire of valor flashes from their eyes. They demand the fight. The tall black ship of the enemy is now close alongside; her tremendous artillery stares them in the face, yawning for destruction. The dreadful fray begins, the air is rent with their horrid thunder. Old ocean trembles and lowers all her waves. The ships are wrapped in flaming fire while storms of iron bullets dash every thing to pieces. The decks are covered with mangled corpses, and the scuppers run torrents of blood."

Not twenty years later, James Fenimore Cooper would write of black ships emerging from mists, and Herman Melville would later write of adventures at sea, putting into the mouths of brave naval officers, such as John Paul Jones, words not unlike these. Jolly and full-throated tars strutted with jolly song on the American stage. Weems had his finger on the pulse of his time. He used the bold bluster of its oratory to comfort, commend, or command.

In a democracy such as Americans enjoy, there is even a kind of pecuniary equality. All men do not make the same in wages or salary, but neither do all men pay the same in tithes and taxes. Suppose, said Weems, as a poor working man, "you own a heavy waggon and a team: with this Jehu-like, you rattle along the highways, tear up the roads, break down the bridges, and set the poor road menders to cursing and swearing, and after all, what is your tax? Why not even a shark skin. But lo! here comes one of the Quality in a little gim-rack Phaeton and Lilliputian pair, not a tythe the substance of your waggon, a carriage that makes no more impression on the road than a cat running over a harpsichord, and yet this gentleman pays a tax of 9 dollars."

Or do you build a comfortable home for less than a hundred dollars—he put the figure at $99.99—there "you and your loving dame with a score of chubby rosy cheeked boys and girls may live merry as crickets, and yet you pay no tax on it, while the rich man in Philadelphia, living in a house that cost $30,000, pays an annual tax of $270. . . . No, no, my brethren," he told them, "if you be really poor, you pay nothing, even though your poverty should be owing to your own shameful love of ease, or of whiskey, you pay nothing."

What though "our good old President," John Adams, has an annual salary of $25,000? It is open to question "whether it is a shark skin too much," for "His Levee, his table, &c. must consume vast sums. It were high treason in him to eat his venison or drink his wine alone. He is expected to act the national Publican, to keep open house and entertain comers from all the winds of Heaven." And consider "the brain wracking, spirit-wasting, hard flesh-consuming study" that must accompany leadership among us: "Look at your Jeffersons, Madisons, Marshalls, Harpers. . . . How many thousands of dollars these men have laid out on their education and libraries to enable them to cope with the long-headed Pitts and Talleyrands of Europe."

And how shall we manifest our gratitude to such people? Certainly not by "splitting into parties and mortally hating one another," describing Jefferson as "an empty pedant, Franklin an old fool, Adams a British agent, and Washington—let faction write the rest!" Then with unashamed fervor, he added, "O my dear Brothers, native or adopted sons of Columbia! if ever a people on earth were under particular obligations to love their country, we are that people." Shall we manifest our gratitude by "splitting into parties and mortally hating one another?"

The Philanthropist ends with an appropriate pious peroration as Weems calls on his countrymen to recognize and cherish one another as equal members of the same body, "as members of one family, journeying together through the chequered scenes of this transitory world, towards a region where all the distinctions of rich and poor, high and low are unknown and where virtue alone shall be exalted and vice degraded forever."

During these troubled years, when Washington, the hero, was retired and the new nation was roiled with quarrels by contending parties, Weems offered a plea for moderation, with love of country replacing love of party or love of section. He became a preacher whose voice was directed toward the whole country, urging peace, patience, and acceptance by each person of the place that God had ordained that he or she should contentedly occupy.

And books would provide him a pulpit from which to speak.

Pohick Church, Dumfries, Virginia

Belle Air, Mason Locke Weems's home in Dumfries.

Panorama of Richmond, Virginia, 1817,
by Peter Maverick, as seen from Mayo's Island.

Popular conception of young George Washington
with his little hatchet beside the ruined cherry tree.

HISTORY,

OF THE LIFE AND DEATH, VIRTUES, AND EXPLOITS,

OF

GENERAL GEORGE WASHINGTON;

DEDICATED
To
MRS. WASHINGTON;

And containing a great many curious and valuable ANECDOTES, tending to throw much light on the *private* as well as *public* life and character, of

THAT VERY EXTRAORDINARY MAN:

THE WHOLE

HAPPILY CALCULATED TO FURNISH A FEAST OF TRUE WASHINGTONIAN ENTERTAINMENT AND IMPROVEMENT, BOTH TO OURSELVES AND OUR CHILDREN.

A wit's a feather, and a chief's a rod;
An honest man's the noblest work of God.

Who *noble ends* by *noble means* obtains,
Or failing, smiles in exile or in chains;
Like good Aurelius let him reign, or bleed
Like Socrates, that man is *great* indeed.

PRINTED FOR THE REV. M. L. WEEMS,
Of Lodge No. 50, Dumfries,
BY
GREEN & ENGLISH, GEORGE-TOWN
(Price 2s. 3d. only.)

Title page of first edition of Weems's *Washington,*
in a pamphlet of 80 pages.

THE LIFE

OF

GEORGE WASHINGTON;

WITH

CURIOUS ANECDOTES,

EQUALLY HONOURABLE TO HIMSELF

AND

EXEMPLARY TO HIS YOUNG COUNTRYMEN

A life how useful to his country led !
How loved ! while living !.....how revered ! now dead !
Lisp ! lisp ! his name, ye children yet unborn !
And with like deeds your own great names adorn.

NINTH EDITION....GREATLY IMPROVED.

EMBELLISHED WITH SEVEN ENGRAVINGS.

—◆+◆—

BY M. L. WEEMS,

FORMERLY RECTOR OF MOUNT-VERNON PARISH.

" The author has treated this great subject with admirable suc-
" cess in a new way. He turns all the actions of Washington to the
" encouragement of virtue, by a careful application of numerous
" exemplifications drawn from the conduct of the founder of our
" republic from his earliest life. No Biographer deserves more
" applause than he whose chief purpose is to entice the young
" mind to the affectionate love of virtue, by personifying it in the
" character most dear to these states."
H. Lee, Major General Army U. S.

PHILADELPHIA:

PRINTED FOR MATHEW CAREY

1809.

By the ninth and definitive edition,
the pamphlet had grown to a 228-page book.

View of the British siege of Charleston, South Carolina.

The heroic Sergeant Jasper replacing the shattered flag
on the ramparts of Fort Moultrie.

Francis Marion and his men crossing the Pee Dee River.

Marion in his encampment in the Santee Swamp,
inviting a British officer to dine on roasted potatoes with him.

William Hogarth's representation of the effects of drunkenness.

"Drunkard's Beware!" was the caption for this illustration
in Weems's *The Drunkard's Looking Glass*.

THE

Drunkard's Looking-Glass.

REFLECTING

A FAITHFUL LIKENESS

OF

THE DRUNKARD,

IN

SUNDRY VERY INTERESTING ATTITUDES;

WITH LIVELY REPRESENTATIONS
OF THE MANY STRANGE CAPERS WHICH HE CUTS
AT DIFFERENT STAGES OF HIS DISEASE;

As first,

When he has only " A DROP IN HIS EYE,"

Second,

WHEN HE IS " HALF SHAVED,"

Third,

When he is getting " A little on the Staggers or so,"

And fourth and fifth, and so on,

TILL HE IS " QUITE CAPSIZED,"

OR,

" Snug under the Table with the Dogs,"

AND

Can " Stick to the FLOOR without holding on."

BY M. L. WEEMS,

Author of the Life of Washington, &c.

SECOND EDITION, GREATLY IMPROVED.

[*Price Twenty-five cents.*]

1813.

Title page of *The Drunkard's Looking Glass.*

GOD'S REVENGE

AGAINST

ADULTERY,

AWFULLY EXEMPLIFIED IN THE FOLLOWING CASES

OF

AMERICAN CRIM. CON.

I. THE ACCOMPLISHED DR. THEODORE WILSON, (DELAWARE,) WHO FOR SEDUCING MRS. NANCY WILEY, HAD HIS BRAINS BLOWN OUT BY HER HUSBAND.

II. THE ELEGANT JAMES O'NEALE, ESQ: (NORTH CAROLINA,) WHO FOR SEDUCING THE BEAUTIFUL MISS MATILDA L'ESTRANGE, WAS KILLED BY HER BROTHER.

BY MASON L. WEEMS,

AUTHOR OF THE LIFE OF WASHINGTON.

THIRD EDITION.

PHILADELPHIA:

PRINTED FOR THE AUTHOR—PRICE 25 CENTS.

1818.

GRIGGS & CO. PRINTERS.

Title page of *God's Revenge against Adultery.*

*Thrice accurs'd CARDS and DICE!
You have been my ruin!*

Frontispiece of *God's Revenge against Gambling.*

"There! G- d D--n You Take That!"
Frontispiece of *God's Revenge against Adultery*.

The Charleston, South Carolina, that Parson Weems knew.

4. ALMANACS, LOVE, AND DELIA

"Ruffled by the Amorous Breezes"

That books sold better than almanacs, indispensable guides for every occasion, telling of times to plant, presenting recipes for milady's kitchen, rates of currency, and lists of elected leaders? For nine pence, a shilling, twelve cents, or even twenty-five a handy household reference book could be obtained, a storehouse of useful information and entertainment. Every family must have one, as a commonplace book, a jest book for entertainment, a diary, and even a schoolbook for children.

The first book published in America is said to have been an almanac, and that in 1639, only nine years after the establishment of the Massachusetts Bay Colony. *The Farmer's Almanac*, first published in 1792, has had continuous circulation ever since. *The World Almanac* has since 1868 provided a rich compendium of useful knowledge to many a household or office library.

Taking hint from popular European almanacs, Benjamin Franklin more successfully than most had raised expectations that, in addition to useful information, each almanac would also provide brisk and edifying instruction such as he provided in his hard-headed instruction on "The Way to Wealth," and the astute sayings of "Poor Richard." Mason Locke Weems was quick to pick up on that.

He had almanacs printed by the hundreds, unashamedly purloining other people's calculations, but adding fillips of his own, and hawking the whole about the countryside under various titles—*The Bachelor's Almanac, The Virginia Almanac*, or to attract a larger group of buyers, *The Virginia and North Carolina Almanac*. Each was much like, often identical to, the other—*The Washington Almanac, The Franklin Almanac, The Grand Republican Almanac*. Not all survive, except as titles, having been used and discarded after service in kitchen, little house, or milady's chamber.

None was more appealing than *The Lover's Almanac* of 1799, containing besides its quota of useful information, "A very seasonable, savoury Dissertation on Love, Courtship and Matrimony—with a most enchanting Flourish on Beauty, admirably calculated to disclose those two most delectable and desirable of all Secrets, how the homely may become handsome, and the handsome angelic."

With no false modesty, Weems admitted to Mathew Carey that this "beautiful treatise on love, courtship and matrimony" was "half fabulous, half real, half my own, and half borrowed." And it sold well. An edition of two thousand copies was gone within a few weeks, and to people of Virginia alone. A year later, he was confident that he could double that figure.

He addressed the "Dear Reader" in introduction: "I am very clear," he wrote, "that our Buckskin Heroes are made of at least as good stuff, as the beef and frog eating gentry on the other side of the water; but neither this nor all our fine speeches to our president, and all his fine speeches to us again, will save us from the British gripe or Charmagnole hug, while they can outnumber us 10 to 1. No, my friend, 'tis population, 'tis population alone, that can save our bacon.

> Let then ye bachelors and ye maïdens fair,
> If truly ye do love your country dear,
> Attend with rapture to the great decree
> Which, thus, in genesis you may see!
> "Marry and rise up soldiers might and main;
> "Then laugh you may at England, France and Spain."

"To press this great duty, at all times necessary, at none more than now, is the object of this almanac. If it should be found to have deserved well of the state, 'twill be well; if it should bring

> To the Clergy, rich licenses,
> To me, little nine pences,

sufficient to splice the main braces, 'twill be still better,—and if the good Angel who keeps the great ledger above, will but credit my good intentions, 'twill be still best of all."

Even the monthly charts of tides and times for planting contained reminders of the compiler's uxorious intention. In January, for example, readers were reminded that "If two sleep together, they have heat, but how can one be warm alone"; in March, "Fast it snows, Loud it blows, But feel no harm, Love keeps us warm"; in April, "Wed for love and work for treasure; O the days of peace and pleasure," and so it continued: "In the month of September, Sweet wedlock remember"; "In October prepare For a sweetheart so fair"; "November take wife And have a sweet life"; and in December, "Weather cold and hard for bachelors."

So the reader is then prepared, after twenty-four pages of useful instruction, to be treated to further discriminating insights into what makes a young woman both desirable and contented as "Exemplified in the History of Miss Delia D——, one of the brightest and loveliest daughters of Virginia." And may, Weems said,

> God prosper long our noble State
> In plenty, love and peace.
> And grant henceforth that bachelor's old
> 'Mongst citizens may cease.

For of "all the sweet passions that dance on the high ropes of the human heart, there is none that comes up to *Love*. Its soft influence is spread over universal nature; and man and beasts, Englishmen and Frenchmen, all own it sovereign. Love surely came down from Heaven, for it ever seeks to refine and raise up every thing thither. It melts the hardest heart, thaws the coldest bosom, enlivens the dullest fancy, beautifies the homeliest face, softens the shrillest voice, sweetens the sourest temper, and enlarges the narrowest soul: And while hatred sinks us into Devils, this dearest of passions exalts us into Angels, and inclines us to every thing that's good.

"A man is never in such fine tune for generous actions as when he is in love; and is hardly ever known to stoop to a dirty deed with the hot fit of love upon him. Nay, the slightest spark of this divine electricity, can melt off the dross of the most savage natures, and transform them into new and amiable creatures.—The Tyger in love forgets his fierceness, and becomes gentle and playful as the Lamb. The scold, that Tygress on two legs, learns to smile, while her tongue loosens its piercing fire-like notes, and lisps soft as the murmurs of the Aolian harp. Even the Miser's flinty bosom is softened, his iron-bound fist is unclinched, and thrusting his hand into his pouch, he produced, O wonder of wonders, a twopence for the beggar. Nay, I doubt not but the Devil himself, were to receive a flash from love's celestial conductor would find hell too hot for him, and instantly re-ascend to his native heaven."

If I were "in a canting mood," Weems continued, "I would down on my marrow bones and hail the living divinity of love—Mighty Cupid!—wonder working God! hear a suppliant's prayer; bend thy bow; draw thine arrows to the very head; let fly in every direction among the unmarried of our land. Let no old maid, no old bachelor escape them. Pierce them to the marrow. Bid them flush and sigh, and dissolve in thy enchanting and delicious fires—lead them in thy silken chains to the temple of Hymen, to the nuptual bower—and then, O ye blest powers who guard the bed of virtuous love! smile on their tender toils—Pour the saving Youth with ruddy cheeks and sturdy frame, around our land:—Inspire them with the love of virtue and of their country—bid them hear the warning word of their beloved President, 'To arms, gallant youths, to arms, nor longer suffer the haughty Gaul to despoil your country's commerce, to beggar her worthiest citizens, and to lead her bravest sons with galling chains.' "

The declaration of this tender passion of love to the object who inspires it, is, he explained, called courtship, and "is generally considered as one of the pleasantest parts of life; because love, hope, desire, and a thousand little amorous cupids, are then fluttering about the heart."

To love that "throws his delicious shafts into our bosoms, from the bright eyes of beauty (either of person or of mind) let me here pay my tribute," said Weems, "to that all-conquering charm—There is nothing that makes its way so point blank to the heart as Beauty. The very first discovery of it throws the spirits into a delicious flutter and makes the eyes sparkle with joy. But of all the dear objects that dazzle the eye, or ravish the soul of man, there is none more to be compared to a fine woman.

> "Search all the flowers that grace the verdant field,
> "Taste all the sweets their fragrant odours yield;
> "Yet those how worthless to the virgin fair!
> "With lovely woman what can we compare?"

Then comes Delia, "the most attractive form that ever graced the world to love."

Delia should be better known. She is the great grandmother of our great grandmothers, the perfect and purified example of what a young lady at the end of the eighteenth century, or perhaps at any time, should and could become. Her beauty, her modesty, her pliant surrender to the joys of wedded love represent, in a peddling parson's perhaps prurient eye, all that is required of a young lady's duty to parents and to love that is pure.

Hers is a portrait that will be recognized—the girl of every young man's parent's dream, who has been and will remain, even in troubled modern times, the model for romance and the tempting auguress of connubial comfort and sweet bedded bliss. Weems wrote what the parents of young girls wanted to believe, and young men also. Delia was, and has remained, the girl of dreams, the model of what in a brave new world a young person might aspire to be. She is trustworthy, loyal, helpful, friendly, courteous, kind, obedient, cheerful, thrifty, brave, clean, and reverent.

She "is the most attractive form that ever charmed the world to love . . . tall and majestic . . . every thing that you can conceive of elegance and exquisite shape. Her soft blue eyes resemble the bright azure of an unclouded sky." Roses and lilies "vie for preeminence in her lovely cheek. . . . Her lovely lips are the prettiest pouters in nature, and look like rosebuds just beginning to blow," and through them, "when opened by a smile that Venus might envy, appear two rows of teeth, even as new shorn lambs, and whiter than the driven snow. The gales from the garden of spices are not sweeter than the breath which passes thro' those portals.

"Around her mouth resides a grace, a sweet enchanting something, approaching to a smile, which like a little fluttering Cupid, just lightens upon you, and after showing a dimple disappears. Her neck is a column of polished ivory, formed by the hand of harmony itself. Her jetty curls full and luxurious, flow with an enchanting negligence down her shoulders, and when ruffled by the amorous breezes are seen to play about her snowy bosom in all the luxury of contrast." She is a woman complete, docile but demanding.

Her excellence is guaranteed by nine "beauty spots," the first of which is her intelligent good sense. All the beauties of Delia's person "are quite eclipsed and lost in the far superior beauties of her mind . . . as far superior to those of the body, as the diamond of Golconda excells in brightness the dull clod of the valley—the beauties of the body fade away like the short-lived flowers; but the beauties of the mind will sparkle when the stars fade away." Indeed, the "beauty of the body often works to its sad disgrace and downfall; but the beauties of the mind . . . by overawing loose desires, prove to a fine woman . . . at once her brightest ornament and best defense."

For "beauties of the body, like the beads and baubles of children, soon grow familiar to the eye, and vary with different climes and different times." To the black, black is beautiful. To the deformed, deformity is no defect. How great "is the goodness of our maker in giving us such different notions of beauty; for if we all tho't exactly alike . . . every man would be in love with the same woman, and every woman with the same man," and envy and hatred would be the result: "What pulling of caps we would have among the ladies, and what duelling and murder among men."

How wonderful it is that "kind heaven, in giving us different tastes, has in a most wonderful manner given us different beauties. The honest rustic thinks himself happy in his strong built Dulcinea—the fine gentleman with his little affected coquette—the common soldier with his dram drinking trull—and the captain with his military mistress."

And fashions will change: "A few years ago a small waist was the high cut of beauty; the ladies then looked like so many wasps, plucked in two by tight lacing." But now, said Weems, in a freer republican age, "this mark of beauty is so entirely hid under their lovely, flowing robes, that a modest man can hardly tell waist at all."

But beauties of the mind remain, and of religion also. "To see this dear girl at church, where she is constantly attendant, is one of the most enchanting sights in nature. In a loose flowing robe, white as snow, set off by her youth and blooming charms, she seems more like an angel," testified Weems, "than anything I ever beheld. Her looks serene and expressive of the respect and gratitude due to the greatest of all good; her

41

features animated by a show of devotion in which she forgets that lovely person which none but herself can forget; her elegant motions, whose gracefulness in others would be a temptation to pride, assume that posture of humiliation due to her Almighty Sovereign; while her bright eyes, which cannot appear in public without kindling the sweetest flutter of admiration and love, are devotedly raised in adoration. Surely those ravishing ideas which we form of Angels were first suggested by some such charming girl as Delia."

Such are the beauties of her mind. No less commendable is her second beauty spot, which is good sense. This "holds the same place to beauty as salt does to cookery; many a dish may be made toothsome without sugar, but none tolerable without salt. So many a woman may be charming without beauty, but no beauty can long be charming without good sense. For want of a little of this animating salt about the brain-pan, many a pretty girl has a silly unmeaning look, and is doomed to sit silent . . . lest by opening the ruby doors of her lips, some ugly thing or other should slip out to spoil her beauty and turn our admiration to contempt."

Take the case of Celia, who, like Delia, is a "masterpiece of beautiful nature," but who is undeveloped even in the commonest of virtues. Her father, "thinking that her beauty could at any time command the best market, paid no attention to her education." Instead of proper schooling, she "was allowed to run wild in the kitchen" among servants, picking up their slovenly words and ways.

"I dined at her fathers," said Weems, where "Celia came out blushing as Fair Rosamund. My heart went pit-a-pat. We sat down to table where it was my fortune to carve a turkey." He turned to Delia, saying, "Madam, shall I have the pleasure to give you a piece of this fowl?" When she nodded assent, he asked, "What part, madam, the wing?" "No," she replied, "I'se no luv Tukky wing. I's luv Tukky bubby."

He wondered then "whether the smell of Tobit's dog-fish

sent the Devil packing faster than such a speech would drive a man of taste from the presence of the prettiest girl in Virginia."

No such "beauty-spoiling vulgarity" ever passed the lips of Delia. "She is gay without *levity*, good without *gloom*, angry without *rage*, neat without *foppery*, modest without *bashfulness*, and well bred without *boldness*: In a word, her good sense enables her to avoid all these improprieties which by showing a weak head or a bad heart, are sure to tarnish the brightest beauty and to make her cheap in our eyes."

And this leads to consideration of Delia's third beauty spot, which is innocence and "sweetly blushing MODESTY," the "*fairest, loveliest* flower of female excellence, without which beauty itself is unlovely and quality contemptible; politeness looks like wantonness, and wit like impudence. The prettiest girl on earth excites our pity and disgust the moment that we learn that she has lost her virtue. In vain may she heave her breast of snow and softly roll her eyes of love; the boasting breath of guilt has passed over her charms, and they are faded."

Weems blushed at the indelicacy of another young lady named Helen, who allowed "a gentleman that is sitting by her to press her knees with his hand, or rudely clasp her in his arms and ravish a kiss from her lovely lips." When "I see her," he said, "displaying her snow-white bosom and panting breasts without even a thin shade of gauze to veil them; or when, to show a fine ancle her petticoat is shortened until half her leg is exposed to sight," he was in "no mood to admire her beauty."

How much to be preferred was Delia, "an entire stranger to the execrable *double entendre*." He had seen and admired her "in company when the ladies had been simpering behind their fans look upon them with sweet childish surprise," wondering what in the world had caused them to affect such confusion.

43

Delia's fourth beauty spot was sensibility: "Not that affected fluff which screams at the sight of a spider, or faints at the agony of a dying fly," but the genuine product "of a heart naturally tender and *exquisitely benevolent* . . . united to all around her . . . with a sister's feeling" that mingled without affectation into the joys and sorrows of others.

"When I have seen her, at the request of her mother, fly to her harpsichord and play with as much spirit as some others would exert to please a young gallant; or when I have seen her beautiful as a princess, kneeling by her gouty father, and with all the tenderness of a young bride helping him on with his shoe; or when I have seen her in high spirits and the best flow of chat, all at once turn serious on hearing the breath of scandal, I have thought if there be any grace which more than another makes a young woman look like an angel, 'tis a sensibility like Delia's."

"Her *meek* and *gentle* SPIRIT," certainly the chief attribute of loveliness, "even in blessed Angels," constitutes Delia's fourth beauty spot, an attribute so "necessary to make a lady truly charming." Delia was not at all like the superficially lovely Hectilia, who though "remarkable for the elegance of her figure, the regularity of her features, and her fine complexion; but for all that, tho' admired by every body," was "beloved by nobody."

Hectilia was "a perfect spit fire whose handsome features" were "entirely overlaid by her ugly passions of pride and ill nature. When I've seen her," testified Weems, "in a fit of good humour, soft and engaging as the doves of Venus, displaying a thousand graces to win the hearts of a large company—and the moment they are gone, her brow darkens, her cheeks grow red with rage, and her eyes flash fire because she has discovered" something so trivial as "a rent in her gown." Or when, "preparing for a ball, unable to satisfy her own vanity, feel over every ornament she put on, quarrels with her maid, with her clothes, her hair, and, growing still more unlovely as she grew more cross."

Delia's "cheeks wear such a perpetual bloom, that the lazy pale-faced belles of the neighborhood will have it that she paints." But it is her temperance and industry that tint her cheeks with a natural red. These compose her sixth beauty spot. "She goes to bed with the innocent lamb, and rises with the chearful lark, to sing her Maker's goodness and to run the pleasant round of domestic duties. . . . The dairy, the manufactory, the garden, her books and her harpsichord are constantly visited by this dear domestic hen.

"Wholesome vegetables, light puddings, and ripe fruits are her favourite food, on which she feeds with delicate temperance. Hence she is blessed with a vigorous constitution, pure blood, high spirits, and fine circulation, which gives bloom to her cheeks and a sparklingness to her eyes," such as "all the catch penny cosmetics on earth could never do.—Yes, the fine vermillion which temperance and industry diffuse over the face of this charming girl, is as far superior to that of art, as the brilliancy of the diamond excells the lustre of French paste, or the ruby hue of the cheek of Hebe, the painted visage of an Haggard Harlot":

> Delia for bloom, on exercise depends,
> If wanting this—no art can make amends.

Her seventh beauty spot is simplicity, for "Delia is an utter stranger to affectation, that bane of female beauty,—not pimples nor freckles, not thick lips nor flat noses, nor all the curses of Cain, were ever half so ugly as affectation."

Consider Elictillia, "a nymph of exquisite beauty," but who, in mimicking the easy graces of Delia "makes herself quite a laughing stock. She comes into a room tottering in her gait like one on stilts; and when she has a mind to be . . . *soft and languishing,* her affected ease is beyond expression unnatural and distrustful."

Having heard that a smile is the mark of beauty, Elictillia is never seen in company "without a ridiculous simper on her face. When she laughs, her lips are . . . drawn as far apart as possible, to shew her fine teeth. Her voice, naturally a good tenor, is screwed out to a squeaking treble. The pout, the languish, the stare, the lisp, and a thousand other incongruities, which in some fine women are highly graceful, because natural, are in her entirely murdered by a silly affectation." But not Delia, who "content in her own loveliness, scorns the meanness and folly of affectation, and shines the fairest daughter of easy, elegant nature."

Delia's cleanliness, which is her eighth beauty spot, "may be, as Aristotle calls it, one of the *half beauties*," though in the intimacies of close affection, testified Weems, " 'tis one of the whole beauties," the "sworn nurse to love." Consider the condition of Miss Kitty who, though pretty, is a slattern, and not a pleasant sight:

> Slip shod her feet, her night gown is unty'd,
> And what she has of head dress is aside;
> She drawls her words and waddles in her pace,
> Unwash'd her hands, and much besniff'd her face;
> A nail uncut, and head uncomb'd, she loves,
> And even shocks us with her dirty gloves.
> O fie, fie, fie!
> Women are made to give our eyes delight,
> A female sloven is an odious sight.

But fair Delia is immaculate, "the dazzled eye can scarcely tell which exceeds, her alabaster bosom or the snow white tucker that shades it." Cleanliness invites simplicity, for true beauty is, "when unadorn'd, adorn'd the most." Delia, "in a plain homespun and a young Quaker's bonnet" seems "a thousand times more attractive than any rich heiress loaded with brocade and jewels."

Her ninth and final beauty spot is politeness, "*beauty's finest polish*, her last finishing stroke, without which her brightest charms would loose more than half their lustre." Weems wrote "loose," not "lose," following fashions in spelling and pronunciation of his day, and thus creating for our day a metaphor more effective than our be-Webstered correctness will now allow. "As a Scotch pebble highly polished," he went on with deliberate plainness, "will pass better than a rough diamond, so a lady of plain features, but of *elegant manners,* will easily win over our hearts from the *prettiest girl* that's *rude* and *ill-bred."*

Consider again the beautiful Celia, who is "lovely as a sunbeam. There needs but a single glance from her sparklers to set a heart on fire." Yet Celia's "abominable rudeness spoils every thing. . . . She giggles and whispers while one of the company is reading or singing. She sniffs an impudent brief reply to questions asked her," treating the questioner "with less respect than a polite woman would show to a slave."

And at table "her rudeness is quite beyond bearing. In silence she feeds voraciously, swallowing such luncheons as are shocking in a lady; at other times she shows a loathing of the best dinner set before her. And what with picking her teeth with her fork, sousing up her nose, picking it with her fingers, blowing it and looking into her handkerchief, I have been so disgusted with Celia, as to think, that if she had the beauty of the sun, she would still be a fright to a man of taste and decency."

But not Delia. "Her politeness is the natural effect of her goodness and good heart." Her "benevolent bosom" finds its "greatest pleasure in pleasing others," a "noble motive, which is ten thousand times sweeter and surer . . . than Chesterfield's system of flattery and dissimulation."

Delia "never interrupts, contradicts, nor slights any that are speaking," treating "her superiors with such an air of cheerful respect, her equals with such complaisance, her inferiors with such affability, and all around with such endearing attention as wins every heart." All of Delia's virtues combine to prove that even

> When the stars and suns shall be nor more
> Shall beauty's graces to their forms restore
> Then, wrought into the soul, let virtue shine,
> The ground eternal, as the work divine.

And this, Weems wrote, is the "End of Dissertation on Beauty."

But not of what he had to say in admiration of the lovely Delia, and the reward that comes to a girl as amiable and talented as she. So he told then, in what he designates as "Chap. II," the "charming history of the tender loves, *delicious Courtship and happy marriage of the youthful Florio and his beloved* Delia," demonstrating "*in the prettiest and pleasantest manner, the obligation of all Ladies and Gentlemen to venture Matrimony, as the sole nursery of mankind—the surest guardian of a young man's* innocence—*the best preservation of his property—the sweetest medicine of Health—the choicest balsam of life—and the delicious Fountain of all the nameless but numerous joy which a tender Friendship and sound love can bestow on a happy couple*":

> Fram'd to give joy, the lovely sex are seen,
> Beauteous their form, and heavenly is their mein;
> The noblest ends the glorious passion sways,
> By love and honor bound, the youth obeys,
> 'Till by his virtues won, the grateful fair,
> Consents in time, to ease her lover's care,
> Seals all his hopes, and in the bridal kiss,
> Gives him the title to untainted bliss.

Delia had not been without suitors. She "was now in the full bloom and ripeness of all conquering eighteen, 'Adorned with all that heaven and earth could give to make her amiable.'—Such charms could not pass unadmired and unadored. Several gentlemen honored her with their addresses, which she declined: but in a manner so tender and *polite*, that instead of lessening, it greatly increased their esteem for her. Looking on a marriage of virtuous friendship as a source of the highest earthly felicity, she was determined never, at least not on the right side of five and twenty, to give her hand when she could not give her heart."

But then came young Florio, "a young gentleman of but slender fortune, but of fine understanding, and remarkably sweet tempered." His "eyes were piercing and lively, his features manly and regular, and his virtues such as to afford a perpetual feast to his fond parents." His father, "a sensibly good old man, who well knowing how much his son's happiness would depend on the choice of a wife," had counselled him: "Happiness, my son, happiness in the married state depends not on riches, nor on beauty, but on good sense, on sweetness of temper, and mutual love" and that beauty, "though so much admired, so much coveted, is a dangerous thing to a young woman. It tends to make her vain." But "the *Graces*, my son," he said, "never loose their influence. At the end of 30 or 40 years, a virtuous wife, who makes an industrious helpmate, a gentle friend and an agreeable companion, charms the husband perhaps more than at first."

Florio "treasured up these valuable hints." With "that picture of a good wife in his mind, he compares it with every woman he sees—'Miss Carlotte is beautiful, but has she good sense—Miss Fanny is sensible, but is she well tempered? She dances elegantly and sings well, but is she not vain of such trifles? Miss Kitty will bring me a clear 5000. but has she not a passion for dreams and pleasure that would out-run the devil were he contestable,' and 'Miss Dorothy is a dear *religious* creature; but is she not too gloomy and superstitious? Is she not too fond of sighing and groaning for a chearful Christian? Will she not often distress herself for fear I shall go to hell, because I would rather read Blair's sermons than Wesley's? Rather go to church than to meeting?' "

49

Florio found none to please him, until he met Delia. His eyes "wandering carelessly over a large circle, soon distinguished and fixed on her." In vain did he reproach himself for rudeness: "His eyes were attracted by a powerful charm." She noticed that he looked at her. She blushed and he blushed, and he tried to turn away, but "sweet emotions, till then unfelt, produced a kind of fluttering in the heart." He became at the same time "more timid and more curious. He was pleased with gazing on Delia, which he could not do without trembling," and "Delia, secretly satisfied with this flattering preference, cast her eyes on him by stealth."

The party over, and each going a separate way, a melancholy descended on both. The "visage of his beloved Delia was deeply engraved on the mind of Florio, and his features were so deeply impressed with that of Delia," that "they both appeared less chearful the rest of the day. A tender sentiment which they did not comprehend themselves, entirely employed their minds in spite of every attempt to divert them." Two days passed, "without seeing one another again, during which time they both experienced a weariness and dissatisfaction in their minds for which they could no way account."

But finally, a "dear welcome moment . . . brought them together again." They talked together, and Florio discovered that beneath Delia's outward charms were "the beauties of her mind, her fine sense and the goodness of her heart." Though true love "is always timorous," Florio finally did manage to open his heart, not in the smooth language of romance, but directly, speaking to the heart.

" 'Charming Delia,' said he, 'I love you; I feel I cannot live without you. I surely may love you without offense; 'tis a tribute to your merit; but may I flatter myself with the hope of some small return.' "

And Delia listened, showing by her "sweetly blushing countenance that she was secretly pleased. She gave him leave to hope, nor did she put his constancy to tedious trial.

The happiness for which she sighed was delayed no longer than was necessary to prepare the ceremony."

When that happy wedding day arrived, that "sweet auspicious evening to which Florio's soul so long had sighed," and "joyful friends were all assembled, the candles lighted, and the clergyman ready to join them in Hymen's bonds," then the "observation that a beauty never looks so beautiful as on her wedding night seemed here to be true. Delia was, if possible, more charming, more dazzling bright than ever." And her gown was "of fine Virginia cotton, white as ermin and beautifully sprig'd with flowers, the whole of it the work of her own fair hands." The happy pair stood happily by as assembled friends sang an epithalamium:

> Hail honor'd wedlock! sacred rite!
>   The crown of life is thine;
> The fountain thou of chaste delight,
>   For Adam's virtuous line,
> Pursuing this, my valued friend,
>   Thou aim'st at highest bliss;
> In Delia's charms thy wishes end,
>   And truth endears the kiss.

And Florio, pressing Delia's hand, "with a look of inexpressible tenderness," sang an extempore celebrating her charm, concluding with fervor,

> I'll kiss thee and press thee till youth is all o'er,
> And then live on in friendship when passion's no more.

"O ye bachelors!" interjected Weems, "ye *barren fig-tree gentlemen,* who are constantly croaking about scolding wives . . . and as constantly whistling the praises of what you call *Freedom,* had you but seen the charming glow (love's fine vermillion) which this song brought into Delia's cheeks, and the melting glance she gave to Florio, you would instantly have acknowledged, that if there be a heaven on earth, it must (religion aside) be found in the union of two such loving hearts."

For "in steering for the port of true happiness . . . the virtuous married man" outsteers the bachelor on every tack, whether it be pleasure, profit, safety, or usefulness, "the four great cardinal points on the compass of life, by which every man, wise or fool, steers his bark," for "matrimony is a rosebud of pleasures a banquet of delights, of which not one stiffnecked bachelor in a thousand may know."

So we leave fair Delia, "adorned with all the charms of gentle beauty, innocence and bloom, reclining like the divinity of love upon her nuptial bed," while borne "on the wings of chaste desire, Florio hastened to the embraces of his sweetly blushing bride."

"Say, now, ye bachelors," Weems challenged, "whether the rapture which this happy youth enjoys in the arms of such Angelic innocence and truth, deserves to be so far insulted as to be compared with the guilty pleasures which the fornicator takes with his dirty, distempered drab.

"Hail wedded love! . . . Here love her golden shafts employs, here lights his constant lamp, and waves his golden wings—here reigns and revels:—not in the bought smiles of Harlots, *loveless, joyless, unendeared.*"

In a final flourish, Weems ends his admonitions with a list of "Pretty Sayings of Maids and Bachelors," reminding them that

> The good or ill hap, of a good or ill life,
> Is the goodness or ill in the choice of a good or ill wife,

and that

> A little house well-fill'd,
> A little land well-till'd,
> A little wife well-will'd,
> Never yet a man kill'd.

Delia, her fair perfections and her glad submission to the gentle joys of wedded love was both mirror and exemplar of what our great grandmother's great grandmothers seem to have been satisfied with seeming to be. How many missed the mark, history begins to reveal, but the model was there, and not just the invention of the well-meaning parson who joined in conspiracy with his fellows, not to create, but to perpetuate a lovely legend that good people wanted to believe. Weems was proud to make her charms more widely known as, travelling through the countryside, he saw to it, as a good salesman should, that just as many of his countrymen as possible would share in admiration of her exemplary virtues.

"Pleasures of the Married State"

The story of Delia had been part narrative and part illustrative exhortation. It had pretended to be a reportorial account, but its principal purpose had been to warn and instruct. It was a sermon garnished with illustrative examples. Weems was fumbling toward a narrative device that in later moral tales he would use with greater ease. If in telling a story, he now seems to ramble, it is not so much that he has an inconsecutive mind as that, in the opinion of most readers of his time, a story must twist and turn to discover some reason for its existence other than being just a story.

Popular fiction hardly anywhere at this time had learned to stand firmly on its own feet as a story told simply for the sake of storytelling. More often than not, it was presented as a tale taken from life, and was meant to point to the dangers of the kinds of things that the tale revealed. Fiction, that is, paraded as fact, and was thought to be the better for that. In so doing, it had reason for being, and that reason was moral and instructive—as the story of Delia had been.

And so, as he prepared a sequel to the story of Delia, Weems interlarded that story with anecdotes and asides that underline its moral intention. What he produced is a narrative shored up with exemplary asides, much as parable had been used in the midst of scriptural injunction. These asides were meant to amuse, but they must also instruct. Amusement was a device to hold the reader's attention until a new flood of instruction inundated him. Weems's narrative method provides a striking example of the way that the pulpit practice of enlivening a sermon with small exemplary narratives worked its way into the writing of fiction as fiction.

As will be seen in his later writings, he will learn to be in better control of the relation between story and instruction. He would then be less discursive, his narrative less fragmented. But both then and now, he had his ear tuned to what people wanted to read, to their attention span, and to their interests and apprehensions. He was of his time, and he represented it faithfully and well.

Delia remained popular, and is suspected to have been separated from her almanac hideaway to appear in a small pamphlet devoted entirely to her exemplary life. But, if she did, that pamphlet, like many of the almanacs, has disappeared, perhaps ripped into curlers for some young lady's tresses or used as slop papers to clean her mother's patty pan. She did appear again late in 1799 in *The Bachelor's Almanac* to play a minor but exemplary role "in a new narrative written," Weems boasted, "by myself." It was called *Hymen's Recruiting Serjeant* and was, he said, "much admired by the best critics of Alexandria where last week I sold a gross in one day and a half."

No copy of *The Bachelor's Almanac* seems to have survived, but, no matter, *The Virginia Almanac for the Year of Our Lord 1800* appeared at the same time, and also contained "Hymen's Recruiting Serjeant," there identified as "the New matrimonial Yankee Doodle for Bachelors, inviting them all, both Big and Small, to look sharp, and with all convenient speed to take unto themselves a Lovely and Loving Wife."

This "new and beautiful dissertation on married life," Weems promised, was "worth a Jew's Eye to all pretty Maids and Bachelors who would live Healthy, and Happy." Then

he quoted the American poet Philip Freneau's certification
that

> 'Tis madness sure, you all agree
> To Lodge alone at thirty three!
> For writings, penn'd by heav'n, have shewn
> That man can ne'er be blest alone.

And to this he added compelling verses apparently of his
own, promising that

> In kindness sure, he far surpasses,
> Who teaches all, both lads and lasses,
> That *Lads* are seldom worth a fig,
> Until they've learn'd of Hymen's jig,
> Nor lasses e'er to bliss obtain,
> Until they've tried sweet wedlock's chain.

And so, he said, "Hurrah for matrimony! that happy state,
which gave us Washington, Jefferson, Adams, Franklin," all
of America's great.

Not many months after it first appeared in the fall of 1799,
"Hymen's Recruiting Serjeant" was taken whole from its
almanac cradle and given a paper cover of its own, thereafter
circulating in edition after edition for twenty years, bringing
more immediate fame to its author then than anything that
he was to write—even more, it may be suspected, than his
protean biography of Washington which in its various ap-
pearances was revised and expanded to meet public taste.

*Hymen's Recruiting Serjeant, or the New Matrimonial Tat-
Too, for all Bachelors* as it was now and thereafter to be
called, required little revision and little expansion. It seems
to have sprung full blown from the contentedly uxorious head
of its creator, who from that time forward was known both
in affection, and in affectionate derision, as the parson who
preached matrimony. Because it illustrates what he seems to
have found most effective in reaching the hearts, and the
pocketbooks, of many of his countrymen, and because it is

no longer protected by copyright, it seems appropriate to do what Weems did in his adaptations of other people's unprotected writings by presenting much of it just as he wrote it. The lightsome but hearty tone to which people responded then is certainly more effective than any wooden paraphrase written by one of their less ebullient descendants.

Weems's formula for persuasion was simple, and is excellently described by Emily E. F. Skeel, who has kept his memory alive by reprinting some of his writings and by helping prepare a bibliography of his works and a record of his correspondence with Mathew Carey. "Take the ingredients of Scriptural admonition and persuasion," explains Mrs. Skeel, and "add thereto a goodly quantity of zestful, highly-tinted vernacular, sprinkle in some verse,—never mind whether they have feet or wings—then stir vigorously with the long spoon of suggestion and allusion, well calculated to get to the bottom of the pot. Who among the sons of men, so reasoned Weems, could resist the heady brew? Its penetrating aroma, its tasty flavor must reach the hidden, secret springs of every right-minded man—for are not such at all times, subject to the sway of reason, ever alert to the direct action between cause and effect? And so we have *Hymen's Recruiting Serjeant*, tooting his way up and down the land and tooting for the 'delicate fair ones' as hard as ever he can."

The little paperback is dedicated "To all the Singles whether Masculines or Feminines, throughout the United States," whom Weems addressed as "dear Gentles," telling them, "I am very clear that our *Buckskin heroes* are made of, at least, as *good* stuff as any of the best of the *beef* or *frog-eating* gentry on 'tother side of the water. But neither this, nor all our fine speeches to our president, nor all his fine speeches to us again, will ever save us from the British gripe, or the Carmagnole hug, while they outnumber us, *ten to one!* No, my friends, 'tis *population alone,* that can save our bacon.

List then, ye Bach'lors, and ye Maidens fair,
If truly you do love your country dear;
O list with rapture to the great decree,
Which *thus* in Genesis, you all may see:
'*Marry and raise up soldiers might and main,*'
Then laugh you may, at England, France, and Spain.

Wishing you all, the *hearing* ear—the *believing heart*—and a
Saving antipathy to *apes*, I am yours, dear Gentles, In the
bonds of Love and Matrimony, M. L. Weems."

And then, as appropriate to a sermonizing parson, the little
treatise is introduced by a passage from Genesis, ii, 18: "And
the Lord said, *It is not good for man to be alone.* No, verily,
nor for the woman either. But what says the preacher? Why,
'*I will,*' says Paul (and Paul, you know, was a sound divine)
'*that the young women marry, and love their husbands; and
raise up children.*' Well said, most noble and patriotic Paul!
May the children of Columbia hearken to thy counsel! that
there be no more old Bachelors in our land, like the scrubby
oaks standing selfishly alone, while our maidens, like tender
vines lacking support, sink to the ground; but that, united in
wedlock's *blest embraces*, they may grow up together as the
trees of the Lord, whose summits reach the skies, and their
branches overspread the nations, making their country the
pride and glory of the earth!

"'*I will that the young people marry,*'" says Paul. "Aye,
that's the point; there let us fix our eyes; There all the
honour, all the *blessing* lies. For . . . If you are for *pleasure*—
Marry! . . . If you prize *rosy health*—Marry! . . . And even
if *money* be your object—Marry." And now, the parson said,
"let's to the point, and prove these precious truths. Draw
near, ye bachelors of the willing ear, while, with the grey quill
of experience, I write" of "the Pleasures of the Married
State."

He used good beer drinking terms as he insists, "Believe
me, citizen Bachelor, never man yet received his *full allow-*

ance head'd up and running over, of this life's joys, until it was measured out to him by the generous hands of a loving wife." How much better than beer in a tavern, where a stout-armed barmaid promises, if she promises at all, only the most transient of pleasures.

And do not mistake me, he warned, "A man, with half an eye, may see that I am not talking here of those droll matches which, now and then, throw a whole neighbourhood into a *wonderation;* where scores of good people are call'd together to eat mince-pies, and hear a blooming nymph of *fourteen* promise to take—*'for better and for worse'*—an old icicle of four score! Or to see the *sturdy glowing youth,* lavishing amorous kisses on the shrivelled lips of his *great-grand-mother-bride!* Oh cursed lust of pelf! From such matches, good Lord, deliver all true-hearted republicans. For *such matches* have gone a great way to make those *sweetest notes, husband and wife,* to sound prodigiously *out-o'-tunish.* The old husband, after his honey-moon . . . grunts a jealous *bass,* while young Madam, wretched in spite of her coach and lute-strings, squeaks a scolding treble; making, between them a fine cat-and-dog concert of it for life!!"

Weems made it clear that he is "talking of a match of *true love,* between two persons who, having *virtue* to relish the transports of a tender friendship, and a *good sense* to esti-mate their infinite value, wisely strive to fan the delightful flame by the same endearing attentions which they paid to each other during the sweet days of courtship." For, "O, if there be a heaven on earth, we must (next to the love of God) seek it in such a marriage of innocence and love!"

And then, in approved homiletic fashion, he examined "the pleasures of the married state" under eight separate headings. The first explores *"the charming society, the tender friend-ship it affords!* Without a friend it is not for man to be happy. Let the old Madeira sparkle in his goblets and princely dain-ties smoke upon his table; yet, if he have to sit down with him, no friend of the love-beaming eye, alas! the banquet is insipid, and the cottager's *'dinner of herbs where love is,'* must be envied.

"Let the pelf-scraping Bachelor drive on alone towards heaven in his *solitary* sulky; the Lord help the poor man, and send him good speed! But that's not my way of travelling. No! give me a sociable *chaise* with a *dear good angel* by my side, the thrilling touch of whose sweetly-folding arm may flush my spirits into rapture, and inspire a devotion suited to the place, that *best devotion*—gratitude and love!!

"Yes, the sweetest drop in the cup of life is a friend; but where, on earth, is the friend that deserves to be compar'd with an *affectionate wife?* that *generous creature,* who, for your sake, has left father and mother—looks to you alone for happiness—wishes in your society to spend her cheerful days—in your beloved arms to draw her latest breath—and fondly thinks the slumbers of the grave will be sweeter when lying by your side! The marriage of two such fond hearts, *in one united,* forms a state of friendship of all others, the most perfect and delightful. 'Tis marriage of souls, of persons, of wishes, and of *interest.*

"Are you poor? Like another *self* she *toils* and *slaves* to better your fortune. Are you sick? She is the tenderest of all nurses; she never leaves your bedside; she sustains your fainting head, and strains your feverish cheeks to her dear anxious bosom. How luxurious is sickness with such a companion. Are you prosperous? It multiplies your blessings, *ten thousand fold,* to share them with one so lovely. Are you in her *company?* Her very *presence* has the effect of the *sweetest conversation,* and her looks, though *silent,* convey a *something* to the heart, of which none but happy husbands have any idea."

As a peddling bookman, often away from home, Weems may be thought to have written with special feeling about leave-taking. "Are you going abroad?" he asks. Then, a good wife "accompanies you to the door—the tender embrace—the *fond, lengthened kiss*—the last soul-melting look—precious evidences of love! these go along with you; they steal across your delighted memory, soothing your journey; while dear conjugal love gives transport to every glance *at home,* and sweetens every nimble step of your glad return. There, soon as your beloved form is seen, she flies to meet you. Her voice is music—the pressure of her arms is rapture, while her eyes, heaven's sweetest messengers of love! declare the tumultous joy that heaves her generous bosom. Arm in arm, she hurries you into the smiling habitation, where, the *fire fair blazing,* and the vestment warm, the neat apartment and delicious repast prepared by her eager love, fill your bosom with a joy *too big for utterance.*

"Compared with a life like this, merciful God! how disconsolate is the condition of the Bachelor! how barren of all joy! Solitary and comfortless at home, he strolls abroad into company. Meeting with no tenderness, nor affection to sweeten company, he soon tires, and, with a sigh, gets up to *go home again.* Poor man! his eyes are upon the ground, and his steps are slow; for, alas! home has no attractions. He sees nothing there but gloomy walls and lonesome chambers. Alone he swallows his silent supper, coils himself up in cold sheets, sadly remembering, that with tomorrow's joyless sun, the same dull round begins again."

Then Weems appended two appropriate songs, presumed to be of his own composing. The first begins,

> In the world's crooked path, where I've been,
>   There to share in life's gloom my poor heart,
> The sunshine that soften'd the scene
>   Was—*a smile from the wife of my heart!*

And the second certifies that

> When fortunes frown, and friends forsake,
>   A loving wife still cheers us;

Our grief or raptures she'll partake;
   Distresses but endears us.

Then he spoke of the second bliss of matrimony, and that is that it *"gives us lovely children to perpetuate our names; to enjoy the fruits of our honest industry, and to derive to us a sort of new existence, which we finally hope will be more prudent and happy than the first.* Ye tender parents! say, what music in nature is equal to that which thrills through your delighted nerves when your little prattlers, with infant voice, attempt to lisp your names!

"See Florio and Delia!" he commanded, a "happy pair! Surrounded by their young ones, blooming as spring—sweet as smiling innocence—and laughter like the *Graces!*—pulling at their knees to catch the envied kiss—while the fond parents with eyes swimming with delight, gaze on them and on each other, filled with gratitude to Heaven for such precious treasures, and daily and gloriously employed in training them up to virtue and happiness. Delightful task! pleasure more than mortal! A pleasure which, according to Moses, the Almighty himself enjoyed when he saw the works of his hands, and saw that all was good. Compared with *pleasures* so *exquisite,* with pursuits so dignified and important as those of the married lady, the amusements of the *single* are, sometimes at least, rather diminutive and girlish."

To illustrate this, he offered the example of Delia, who "was lately visited by a wealthy old maid, a cousin of her's, who entertained her with a world of chat about her diamond necklaces, gold ear-rings, and so forth, which she displayed with great satisfaction. She was scarcely done, before Delia's children, returning from school, ran into the room with blooming cheeks and joy-sparkling eyes, to kiss their mother. Delia then, with all the transports of a happy parent and echoing Cornelia on the Gracchi of classical Rome, exclaimed, *'There, my dear cousin, are my jewels, and the only ones I admire.' "*

What a "glorious speech!" Weems exclaimed. "Worthy of an American lady! For those living ornaments which give to our country plenty in peace and security in war, add a brighter lustre to the fair, than all the sparkling jewels of the East."

Then he called on biblical authority, history, and recent events to drive home his points. He quotes Jesus, of course, who said, *"Suffer the little children to come unto me, and forbid them not; for of such is the kingdom of God."* Then he reminded readers of the prime minister of Agesilaus who came upon "that great prince in high romp with his children," and who would join the romp until Agesilaus told him that he could not comprehend such play because he was not a parent: "A fond parent finds . . . something *wonderfully improving* in the society of his children."

And he spoke of "that French Hannibal, Bonaparte, (who is a married man)," who when his forces were advancing on the Austrians, saw two little children cringing nearby, crying with fright "at the sight of so many dreadful faces" advancing all around them. He thereupon halted his troops, moved the children from danger, and only then motioned his troops forward: "They raised the song of war—(the Marseilles' hymn)—the song of heroes fighting for their *hoary sires*, their weeping wives, and helpless babes," and the Austrians "fell before them, as the fields of ripe corn fall before the flames that are driven on by the storms of Heaven."

After such a thunderous peroration, he closed this section on the second bliss of matrimony with three songs written by Florio to Delia in thankfulness for, among other things, the three "pledges of our mutual love" that their marriage had produced—just as Weems's marriage had earlier in that year produced his third child, and first son. Indeed there is much throughout *Hymen's Recruiting Sergeant* to suggest that Weems was celebrating newfound joys of his own. And what he found, he would share with his countrymen, and women also. He spoke from his own experience, his own heart, his own contentment.

The third bliss of matrimony was, he testified, that it "increases the pleasure of defraying family expenses." And again, he turned to authority: " 'Where love is,' said the great William Penn, 'there is no task; or, if there be, the task is pleasant.' " He admitted that to "part with money is oft'-times a hard task, *a bitter pill!* nothing but love can gild it completely."

He told then the exemplary tale of an old bachelor, "who, from the vulgar error that a wife is an expensive piece of furniture, kept house for himself," did his own shopping, but when forced to pay for what he had bought, "dragged up his purse . . . as reluctantly as ever poor rogue haul'd off his doublet to receive Moses's law from the twining cow-hide."

But Florio found "the purchases of conveniences for his family" to be "one of the sweetest luxuries of life." How happy is Delia when he brings her a present. And "what transports will our dear little ones be thrown into! what sparkling eyes! what rapturous kisses" when some knick-knack is bought for their delight.

The fourth bliss of matrimony is that " *'Tis the only money-making state!"* The good Lord did not put "ladies here to be . . . *pensioners,* but . . . *help-mates."* Those young sparks "who are pleased to think of a wife as an *elegant play-thing,* intended only to *dress* and *dance, visit* and *spend money,"* should consider the "picture of a good wife, drawn by the pencil of Solomon, (with a touch or two of the American brush)," from Proverbs, xxxi, 12–24: "Behold a virtuous woman, for her price is above rubies."

12. She riseth with the day, and prepareth breakfast for her household; yea before the sun is risen she hath her maidens at work.

13. She seeketh wool and flax, and layeth her hand willingly to the spindle, while her right hand merrily turneth the wheel.

14. She looketh well to the way of her family, and eateth not the bread of idleness.

15. She regardeth not the snow; for her household are clothed in *fearnought*.

16. By her much industry her cheeks are made ruddy like the rose of Sharon; yea, her nerves are strengthened, so that when she heareth talk of the hysterics, she marvelleth thereat.

17. Her house is the habitation of neatness, so that the heart of her husband is refreshed when he entereth into her chamber.

18. She maketh fine linen, and selleth it, and delivereth much cloth to the merchants.

19. Her husband is known in the gates by the fineness of his apparel, for she maketh him cloathing of silk and purple.

20. Her turkey cometh in plenteously in his season, and the fat duck, yea, also the green goose is oft-times seen self-basted at her spit.

21. Her poultry multiplieth exceedingly in the land, even as the black-birds in the corn-field for multitude; so that she feedeth her household daintily on chicken pies.

22. Her kine are fat, and well favoured. They know not of the hollow horn; for while the winter is yet far off, she provideth them an house; their rack is filled with hay; and their manger lacketh no food; hence her dairy is stored with milk, and her firkins with choice butter.

23. Her children rise up and call her blessed; her husband also, and he praiseth her.

24. She will do him good and not evil all the days of her life. And "now citizen bachelor," he asked, "will you any longer talk about *maintaining* such a wife as this! And such a wife every *good girl* in America will make, if married to the *lad* of her heart."

Consider the case of Mr. Goodrich of Portsmouth, Virginia: "What sea has not been ploughed by his numerous keels? And yet Mr. Goodrich owed it all . . . to a *good wife*. While a bachelor, he worked hard and made money, but it was all soon squandered on frolicking and grog. At twenty-two he married a girl, poor in wealth, but rich in *love, industry* and *health*. For the sake of her he instantly quitted his old tippling companions and prodigality. He possessed in the world but one . . . flat (a large open boat) in which he coasted along up the James river to the mouth of Nansemond, 14 miles, for oyster shells to Portsmouth and Norfolk, happy as a prince, when he was returning his load, to see his dear girl. In a couple of years he picked up enough to buy another boat," and then after "carrying on their oyster shell trade for some years . . . they purchased a *little shop,* afterwards a *store,* and in about thirty years, they had as many as fifteen sail of vessels at sea!"

But when it came to "that great fortune-making virtue, *frugality,* the good Lord have mercy on the Bachelors! for there is not one in ten of them who has so good a notion of it as a *monkey;* for thrifty Jacko will put away the balance of any good *nugs* that he happens to fall in with; but among young Bachelors, the eternal cry is, *Who will show us any fun Hurra,* for the *horse-race,* the *cock-fight,* the *billiard-table,* or the *bagnio.* Dash go the dollars! the hard scrappings, and tight savings of a poor old father's life.

"This *glorious* youth is soon seen sneaking along with the sheriff; his creditors fasten upon him, and pick him to the bone. Choused out of his estate, and ashamed to lift up his booby face, he stalks among his *rich relations,* on whom he has the honour to be billetted for life." Such "is the end of many a *green-horn,* who runs into bad company and ruin for want of a beloved wife."

Not so with Florio: "His Delia, and his sweet little prattlers constitute his circle of happiness. For their sakes . . . he studies every art of economy, and is getting rich fast."

And here Weems interjected a somewhat racier moral tale: "A good old gentleman, a *Friend,* driving along one morning through a certain street in Philadelphia, saw his son sneaking out of a *brothel!* Young hopeful, having a quick eye, caught the venerable form of his father, and instantly slunk back, confused. The old gentleman order'd his coachman to stop at the door, and call'd out, '*Isaac! My son! My son! Never, while thee lives, be asham'd to come out of a bawdy-house; but, forever be ashamed to go into one.*' "

Weems, however, would not place all blame on the son. Addressing the father, a Quaker and therefore in the popular mind, a penurious man, he says, "Had thee, like Abraham of old, but sought out for thy son some lovely *Rebekah*, some *sweet loving wife*, to comfort the young man, there would have been no need to chase him out of a *bawdy-house*." For, as St. Paul had said, "*The love of money is the root of all evil; which while some covet for their children, they suffer them to err from the path of innocence.*"

Weems thus reminded his readers among the country folk, and the city folk also, of the American South of some of the sophisticated chicaneries to be found in the large cities of the North. He appropriated one of the increasing number of anecdotes that circulated about Benjamin Franklin, in which "a gentleman of Philadelphia said to the old Doctor, '*Neighbour Franklin,*' he said, '*I have made, to-day a run of excellent small beer; can thee tell me how to preserve it; for my poor neighbours, some of them are rather too fond of my small beer? Why,*' replied the Doctor, '*I believe there's nothing like clapping a pipe of good wine beside it.*' "

And that proved, said Weems, that a man "can hardly be one of the *elect*, who can leave the *pure nectar* of a dear wife's embraces, for the accursed cup of a harlot's arms." No wonder some members of his congregation were said to find his sermons often filled with nonsequiturs better in sound than sense.

The fifth bliss of matrimony is that it "*excites the noblest virtues.* The man who truly loves his wife, desires, above all things, to be loved by her. . . . Yes, a fond husband has an infinite advantage over the old Bachelor, a tenfold animation to every thing great and good. He anticipates the raptures of his beloved family on hearing of his noble actions, and the high respect which a grateful public will pay them for his sake. And, on the other hand, the very thought of a base action startles him," as he considers "its dreadful effect on his wife and children! He sees them *drowned in tears*, hanging their heads, and ashamed to go into company forever after." If, he said, "it be the will of Heaven that my children be poor, let them inherit an *honest* poverty, and let their little cottage be cheered with the sweet beams of innocence."

And marriage keeps youth safe from the clutches of the harlot. That is its sixth gift of bliss. " 'Tis heaven's decree," Weems explained, "that the race of man shall be kept alive by the union of the two sexes. To render that union certain," God "cropt a twig of *love* from the tree of life, and planted it in the human bosom. This sweet passion, wisely directed (to wedlock) is a source of the purest satisfaction; but degenerating into brutish lust, it hurries the poor deluded youth into dangers, and evils, the very thought of which is enough to make a parent tremble."

Consider the case of young Eugenio. "Alas! poor Eugenio! Eugenio was the handsomest young bachelor Carolina ever boasted." He had a fortune of £10,000 and a liberal education. "In the full bloom of twenty-three, he went out to London to complete his studies of the law. At the play-house he was ensnared by the fatal charms of a beautiful harlot, in whose distempered arms he met destruction. Bitter were his lamentations, when he found that no medicines could cure, and that all his own, and the fond hopes of his friends were blasted forever. He returned a mere skeleton to Carolina, and there died in the arms of his broken-hearted parents. Thus short was the life, thus miserable the end of one who was entitled to match with any of the finest women of America."

And matrimony preserves many a young man *"from black eyes and broken heads.* If lust has slain its thousands of inconsiderate bachelors, anger has slain its tens of thousands.

. . . *Our sex,*" explained Weems, "is hard and unloving, too fond of quarrelling and throat-cutting. Lovely woman was given to soothe and soften; and verily, the young man who walks without one of these charming guards, *walks in jeopardy every hour.*"

Consider the case of Draco, a young bachelor. "For amusement-sake he often strolls to a tavern, whither he carries with him the ill-temper he got from nature, increased by habits of tyrannizing over little negro slaves. He soon falls in with young men as self-will'd and passionate as himself. Contradictions lead the van! contentious fellow! abuse succeeds contention! and blows, black eyes, and broken heads bring up the rear.

> Great God! on what a slender thread
>   Hangs a man without a wife!
> Untimely of by *lust or hate,*
>   He ends his wretched life!
>
> Dangers stand thick through all the ground,
>   To raise the Bach'lor's tomb;
> And fiercest passions wait around,
>   To drive the sinner home.

"It was once hoped," said Weems, "that the religion of *love* founded by Christ would have preserved our young Bachelors from these hateful passions; but that religion has rather lost ground among people of *weak heads.* Such, however, still have hearts; and all hearts are within the reach of the *ladies.* Their sweet looks and gentle manners may yet recover" those bachelors "to humanity.

"How often have we seen, that when a company of wrangling Bachelor-politicians had worked themselves up into redness and rage, threatening battle royal, the sudden entrance of a fine girl has instantly called them to order, and made the old heroes look as sweet and smiling as so many bride-grooms. Now, gracious heaven! if a single glance from lovely woman can thus turn *passion* into *peace, fury* into *friendship*, what may not be expected of the happy man who is married to one of these all-refining charmers?"

See Florio and Delia. "Married to Delia, the gentlest of her sex," Florio's temper was "sweetened and his manners polished, by his passions for her." He "gradually, as is the *nature* of love, falls into an imitation of those gentle virtues he so highly admires in her. These graces, thus naturally learned from her, he carries with him into the circle of his acquaintance, where they make him dear to every body. Hence, when he takes leave of Delia in the morning to go into company, her tender bosom is not alarmed that he will come home at night with a black eye or broken head, or be brought in a corpse murdered in some bloody fray. No, No; thank God, she knows that he is safe; she knows that he loves and is beloved by every body. 'Tis to this amiable wife that Florio is indebted for much of his engaging manners." *She* taught him

> To feel the generous passion rise,
> Grow *good by loving, mild* by *sighs.*

The final bliss of matrimony is that it "preserves a young man from that worse than hellish practice, duelling. 'The single state,' says Dr. Johnson, 'has no joys.' *No wonder* then," said Weems, that "so many young fools with hot livers and fiery bloods, are in such a passion to be quit of it. But the case is very different with him whose life is happy, and who has such strong ties (a dear wife and children) to attach him to it."

Consider once more the example of Florio and Delia. " 'I have often wondered,' said Florio, 'how a married man can ever be tempted to fight a duel. When I am sitting with Delia, surrounded by my *romping, laughing* little ones, those precious parts and members of myself, who hang on me not only for the tenderest joys of life, but for bread and protection, I feel my life so inestimably valuable, that to sport with it and risk it in a duel, appears to me the most horrid crime that I could possibly commit. If I am but slightly disposed, Delia is wretched; were I in a duel to get shot through the head, and to be left on the field weltering in blood, is there a tongue on earth that could tell her the tidings! What would become of my poor deserted orphans? Who, like their *parent*, would press them to his bosom, dry their tears, bear with their infirmities, supply their wants, and thus lead them through the paths of virtue here, to endless happiness thereafter.' "

Then Weems breaks into a paean of praise of the holy state of matrimony: "O blessed matrimony of *Prudence* and *Love!* What tongue can tell thy benefits to *Man?* Instituted of God in Paradise, honoured of Christ by his first miracle; you still convert the desert into Eden, the commonest water into the richest wine. Reuniting man to his other *half,* you restore him to his *natural,* his *dearest* friend. Calling him from the deadly haunts of harlots, gamblers and duelists, you lead him into the peaceful circle of his beloved wife and children; there you harmonize his passions, sweet his temper, and by inspiring him with the love of innocence and of virtue, you give him to taste the purest felicities of this life and prepare them to drink of those rivers of love and joy which flow at God's right hand for ever more."

Then, lowering his voice, he spoke with confident ease and persuasive confidence. "O generous parents! natural guardians of your children! Encourage them to marry, to marry early .'Tis the voice of all *wisdom, human and divine.*

"What says God himself? ' *'Tis not good for man to be alone.'* Then least of all for a young man.

"What says Solomon? *'My son, rejoice with the wife of thy youth and let her be as the loving fawn and pleasant roe; for why, my son, wilt thou embrace the bosom of a harlot, whose way is the way of hell, going down by the chambers of death.'*

"And what says the American Solomon? *'Early marriages are the best; they settle young men and keep them out of bad*

company and connections, which too often prove their ruin, both in mind, body and estate.'

"And if after *Solomon* and *Franklin*, we dare mention Common Sense. What says *Common Sense?* Why *Early Marriages are best.* They *fix*, on youth, the *virgin passions*, which if suffered to wander from *beauty* to *beauty*, contract at length such a *taste* for *variety*, that though married at last to the most elegant woman on earth, she would find her arms deserted for those of a cook-wench!!!"

Then he paused to praise those simple democratic virtues of simplicity, hard work, thrift, and prudence. "For sweet heaven's sake," he pled, "let us cease to educate our children as *fine Ladies* and *Gentlemen*. . . . This most unfortunate practice has strangled more matches, and propagated more vice and misery than any other. By bringing up your son to be ashamed of work . . . to affect the airs, company and pleasures of the great . . . you do him the *greatest* of all possible injuries. You cut him off from the happiness of marrying the woman he loves, though bright and good as an angel, *if she have no money.*

"And you set him on all the crimes and curses of courting, cringing and lying to the woman *he loves not*, just for the sake of her land and negroes; and after trotting up and down the country with a negro-fellow and portmanteau at his tail, courting every rich old body that he can hear of—knocking about like a shuttle-cock, backwards and forwards from widow to maid, and from maid to widow—Now by a smile vaulted up to the highest ceiling of hope; then, by a frown, tumbled on the hard floor of despondence: to-day, blest as an angel, in full prospect of marrying a *fine fortune*—to-morrow, cursed as a demon, at seeing his girl and guineas born off by a hated rival.

"Thus after running the gauntlet, between *sour-looking fathers, bridling mothers,* and *haughty jilting daughters,* for ten or fifteen years perhaps, the poor wretch is further from

a fortune than he was at first. Nay, grey, wrinkled, and ugly—over head and ears in debt—dunned by creditors—depressed in spirits—hail fellow well met with gamblers, pickpockets, highwaymen, horse thieves, and duelists, he takes refuge in hard drinking, turns desperate, and from extremity of wretchedness, blows out his brains, or compels justice to hang him up like a dead dog despised!!!

"O for God's sake, and as you prize your son's happiness, train him up to . . . habits of industry, and give him a *good profession* or *trade*. This will soon put him in the way to maintain a family. . . . In the full bloom of *twenty-one*, with a mind pure as unsun'd snow, chaste and delicate as an angel, he clasps the yielding maid. Love and conscious innocence exalt their joys to raptures! And while the fortune-hunter is anxiously trotting up and down, to and fro in the earth, like another poor de--l seeking what wealthy maid or widow he may devour, our Florio and his Delia, like Milton's happy pair, *'emparadis'd in each other's arms, enjoy their fill of bliss on bliss.'* "

Yes, Florio and Delia, "by waiting might have married some rich old bodies, with negroes, land and chariots, to make a noise in the world; but what's the world to them, its pomps, its vanities, and its nonsense all, who in each other clasp every virtue that can insure competence and bliss? They feel the generous wish to surround each other's dearer self, with all this life's comforts; to these, love gives the flavour of dainties. They *feel, 'that better is a dinner of herbs, where love is, than stall-fed beef, and hatred therewith.'* "

But, asks "the fortune-hunting bachelor, 'Is not . . . the education of children confoundedly expensive and heavy on a poor fellow?' Yes, if that poor fellow chooses to play *the fool* and *miseducate* them. If he choose his daughter to spend her time in reading novels, lying a-bed, mimicking the fashions, trailing her silks, and playing the *fine lady*, he'll find her expensive enough, aye, and *long* enough too, I'll warrant. And

if he is for bringing up his son for a fine gentleman, dressing like a jay, cantering away to horse races, betting on old tricks, drinking and blustering at taverns, he'll find him abundantly expensive; and after all his toil and trouble to maintain this fine young gentleman of a son, he must be constantly getting between him and the sheriff, giving bail of some sort or other. Children thus educated are the heaviest cross, cost, and curse of a man's life.

" 'But my children,' says Florio, 'are my *wealth*. My love for them and their dear mother, called forth that industry and economy which first gave me property, and now they improve it. They affect not the trifling part of *fine ladies,* but the high character of *useful women.* Their dear fingers milk our cows, make our butter, spin and weave our apparel, prepare our food, beautify our house with flowers, and render us a thousand important services; while our *sons,* one of them manages our farm, another superintends our mill, and a third keeps our store. *Love* sweetens their service—parental affection enhances its value, and their tenderness and fidelity afford us a perpetual delight.' Happy parents who have such *dear children* to *govern!* Happy children who have *such parents to obey!*

"Dear Bachelors," said Weems in conclusion, "My willing pen has, for an hour past, been pouring these delightful truths over the preceding pages, and yet . . . I look back and see what a noble tide of arguments in favour of conjugal bliss I have yet to pour down upon you, to wash out the leprous stains of old Bachelorism; and extinguish, if *possible,* the pestilence of celibacy.

"Yes, I have yet to run out upon you . . . another and *heavier* of *obligations* to marry—Obligations founded on the mighty base of goods, *national, universal,* and *eternal.* I have not yet shown you, that if you love the *Creator,* you ought to marry, to make his creatures *happy*—that if you love *mankind,* you ought to *marry,* to perpetuate the glorious *race*—

74

that if you love your *country*, you ought to *marry*, to raise up soldiers to defend it—in fine, if you wish well to *earth* or to *heaven*, you ought to marry to give good citizens to the one, and glorious angels to the other.

"To these *sweet persuasions* to wedlock, dear Bachelors, I could add many others of a rougher aspect. I could tell you what the great legislators of all nations have thought of *old Bachelors*, and how cheap they have held them; I could tell you what *broad hints* of disapprobation were shown them by those mighty republicans, the *Greeks* and the *Romans*; how they jeered and jested, taxed and tormented; how (degraded to *wood-cutters* and *water-pumpers*, to *scavengers* and *watchmen*) they were obliged to cleanse the streets, and bawl the time of night! while the justly *privileged* and happy *married men* fondly clasp'd in beauty's arms, were spending the downy hours in sweet connubial bliss, but I spare you."

The sermon ending, he pronounced a benediction: "May the words which you have at this time read with your *outward* eyes, make such an impression on your *inmost* feelings, that you may, soon as convenient, renounce the sorrows and insignificance of celibacy, and assume the *dignity*, the *usefulness*, and *joy* of the married state! *Then*, and not till then, shall you find the true relish of your *fatted calf*; your water shall be turned into wine; the throbbings of your bosom shall be quieted; and, happier than the penitents of old, you shall have rejoicings over you, not in *Heaven* only, but also on the earth.

> I am married and happy. With wonder hear this,
>   Ye rovers and rakes of the age,
> Who laugh at the mention of conjugal bliss,
>   And whom only loose passions engage.
>
> You may laugh, but believe me you're all in the wrong,
>   When you merrily marriage deride
> For to marriage the permanent pleasures belong,
>   And in them we can only confide.

. . . .
If you ask me, from whence my felicity flows?
  My answer is short—*from a wife;*
Whom for *cheerfulness, sense* and *good nature* I chose,
  Which are beauties that charm us for life.

To make home the seat of *perpetual delight,*
  Ev'ry hour *each* studies to seize,
And we find ourselves happy from morning to night,
  By—*our mutual endeavours to please!*

And then with a bow and flourish, he left his paper pulpit "Wishing you every felicity that *lovely* wives and beauteous babes can afford to gentlemen of *sensibility* and *patriotism,* I remain, dear Bachelors, Your very sincere friend, M. L. Weems." The words of his mouth and the meditations of his uxorious heart have revealed much of the mores of our ancestors, what they did and what they were warned against doing.

The distribution among them of *Hymen's Recruiting Serjeant* in edition after edition over many years, as perhaps young America's first best selling popular paperback, provided a formula for reaching the hearts and pocketbooks of readers over many years. Delia becomes Elsie Dinsmore or the girl of the Limberlost and a thousand others besides, and Florio is all the valiant young men who in high stiff collars or open shirts continue in honest endeavor.

Parson Weems, the marrying parson, he was there, if not the first, certainly among the foremost.

And among the most active also. Just pushing into his forties, he seems to have been at the peak of his vigor. Not only was he writing books that would sell, he was hawking them, and others also, preaching as he went, if only to draw crowds to whom books might be sold. He affected special pride in having convinced Mathew Carey, a Roman Catholic, to print a handsome new edition of the Protestant Bible. "Up and down the country we go," he said with some swagger in the words, "preaching and selling bibles."

He kept his church at Pohick as long as he could, and also, he said, did "much preaching and praying up and down the country," in Virginia and Maryland, collecting money for the establishment of a charity school in his parish. His preaching reached far, and his reputation spread wide. One fair mulatto girl of seventeen, sitting in a corner of a log tavern in dalliance with a young countryman, was overheard to say that "if Parson *Wems* preaches, I wouldn't go. He always preaches up matrimony."

One Sunday morning early in the century, the little church at Pohick was visited by John Davis, a young English man of letters who was to become something of a legend-preserver himself by incorporating into his novel, *The First Settlers of Virginia*, the story of John Smith and Pocahontas. The church-yard hummed with activity, Davis reported, "the rattling of carriage wheels, the crackling of whips," and the church bell "suspended to a tree a few yards from the church" calling the people to service. "But the discourse of Parson *Wems* calmed every perturbation. For he preached the great doctrines of salvation, as one who experienced the power." He "felt what he said; and indeed so uniform was his piety, that he might have applied to himself the words of the prophet, 'My mouth shall be telling of the righteousness and Salvation of Christ all the day long; for I know no end thereof.' "

The congregation, Davis observed, was "about one half . . . composed of white people, and the other of negroes," among whom "were to be discovered the most satisfying evidences of sincere piety; an artless simplicity, passionate aspiration after Christ; and an earnest endeavour to do the will of God." After the service, Davis asked Weems his opinion of the piety of the blacks. " 'Sir,' said he, 'no people in this country prize the Sabbath more seriously than the poor trampled upon negroes. They are swift to hear. . . . They are wakeful, serious, reverent, and attentive to God's house; and gladly embrace opportunities of hearing his word. Oh! it is sweet preaching, when people are desirous of hearing! Sweet feeding the flock of Christ, when they have so much appetite.'"

And then the parson turned to the visitor to ask, "How, Sir, did you like my preaching?" To which Davis replied, "Sir, it was a sermon to pull down the proud, and humble the haughty. I have reason to believe that many of your congregation were under spiritual and scriptural conviction of their sins. Sir, you spoke home to sinners. You knocked at the door of their hearts."

"I grant that," Weems is said to have replied, and then, somberly shaking his head, added, "But I doubt . . . whether the hearts of many were not barred and bolted against me."

Later in that year, which was 1801, he being so often away on his bookselling routes, his congregation appointed another clergyman in his place. But then, the next summer, he "listened," he said, "to the impunities of my old . . . parishioners, to preach to them once a fortnight" until the end of the year. After that, though he often presided over services in neighboring churches, he seems only infrequently to have stood in the high-raised pulpit of the old Pohick church.

But his preachings continued, at the portals of courthouses, at the doors of taverns, at racing days and at country fairs, and at public sales where goods or Negroes were up for auction. "I am obliged to preach very often," he said, sometimes four times a week, "in order to get the people together." He preached "the example and virtue" of George Washington, with his book on the late President held high in hand, offered as a permanent reminder of that virtue and that example. And he preached the gospel also, and how its strictures were emphasized in the moral tracts that he offered for sale, interspersing what he said with quips and anecdotes, and, if tradition is to be believed, with occasional mild ribaldries to keep his listeners alert.

He was increasingly in demand at weddings, known as the

marrying parson whose blessing guaranteed a happy conjugal life. "Thank God," he said, "my two books on marriage (the happiness of) have caused me to be sent for, far and near, the grand Porter of the Hymeneal Vestibule. Their douceurs of gratitude," he said, "this week (grace au dieu) makes me nearly 50 Dolls."

And he presided at funerals, speaking sometimes with such grace and fervor that he was tempted to make what he said more widely available. His remarks on the death of a worthy lady of Fairfax received "from first rate good judges much commendation of it as bids me to set it to press." He thought of calling it *The Lovely Wife*, and asked Mathew Carey to find for him "a *superlatively lovely female likeness*" that he might use as a frontispiece. But nothing is discovered to have come of that.

He seems to have been kept continuously busy. "By Christmas," he wrote in May, 1801, "I shall have received 500 Dol. from 3 churches, fees Hymeneal & funeral." And two weeks later, he wrote to Carey, who wondered why he was not on the road selling books, that the "Prospect of Nuptials, of a pair of my most respected parishioners has kept me at home." And as he travelled, young couples in outlying towns or villages seem increasingly to have called on him to assist in promoting what he considered to be the first step in God's plan for providing the new nation with sturdy soldiers and tillers of the field.

During these early years of the century the selling of Bibles seems to have been his most profitable enterprise. It amused him that he had successfully enticed the Roman Catholic Mathew Carey into the printing of Protestant Bibles, and with such rich returns: "If due attention be paid, you may," he assured the printer, "monopolize the Bible business of America." Sales of that book alone could bring in a handsome income, as much as $15,000 or even $20,000 a year: " 'Tis a good thing to be on the back of a good whale, that will keep us up," he said, "and, after all, land us Jonah like, safe on heaven's dry shore at last."

Meanwhile, as a kindly physician, he suggested to Carey that through the fever-ridden days of August he fortify himself with "a little bark daily; good Port, no alcohol—weak tea or coffee well milkd, 3 cups, no more." That might keep their relation more friendly.

And so, with joshing and quarreling, with expectations far beyond what bookselling in the early 1800s could satisfy, the partnership between these two continued. There were delays and recriminations on both sides, and Weems was sometimes forced to languish at home for lack of immediately saleable stock. "I long to be," he complained, "among the Bible loving people of the North." But when he got there, his gig well loaded, he found that the selling of Bibles to the pious people of western Pennsylvania was like attempting to sell icicles to Eskimos. Almost every family had at least two, and one Quaker family had seven. "But I hope that at my preaching appointments of which I have a fine train," he wrote, "I shall pretty well get rid of my cargo." And, if tradition is to be believed, he almost always did.

6. THE WASHINGTON CONNECTION

"I Did Cut It with My Hatchet"

Weems acted quickly on his suggestion to Mathew Carey that they undertake the publication of a series of small biographies of American heroes by beginning one himself. In June, 1799, he wrote that he was preparing and had "nearly ready for the press, a piece christened, or to be christened 'The Beauties of Washington.' Tis artfully drawn up," he added, "enlivened with anecdotes, and in my humble opinion, marvellously fitted" to the taste of his countrymen. "What say you to printing it for me?" It would be small, paper covered, and would "sell like flaxseed at a quarter of a dollar. . . . I could make you," he promised, "a world of pence and popularity by it."

But meanwhile he had been employed with other things—occasional pastoral duties at Dumfries, wearisome travelling, and the writing of *The Philanthropist*, the story of the beauties of Delia, and *Hymen's Recruiting Serjeant*. That year at the end of the eighteenth century had been a busy year indeed, and Weems, unbeknownst, stood on the threshold of fame.

George Washington, retired from the presidency to his estate at Mount Vernon, was at the peak of his popularity. He had guided the country through its first years of independence, and almost everyone thought that he had guided it well. He had, in the large, kept himself free from conflicting political ideologies. Now, as John Adams and Thomas Jefferson continued to lead contending parties, each attempting to determine how the new nation should be governed, he sat serenely back, his work well done, a Cincinnatus retired to his flocks and fields, in a very real sense first in the hearts of his countrymen. His death in December, 1799, brought forth such a shower of sorrowing song and sermon as had hardly ever, anywhere, mourned the death of a statesman before then. His birthday was pronounced a day of public mourning, and was to be a national holiday forever thereafter.

For years he remained the national hero, until after the Civil War, when he was partially eclipsed by Abraham Lincoln. Forty years after Washington's death, Henry David Thoreau recorded that for him, "It is his erectness and persistency that attract. A few simple deeds with a dignified silence for background and that is all. He never fluctuated, nor lingered, nor stooped, nor swerved, but was nobly silent and assured. He was . . . as much respected as loved. His instruction to his steward—his refusal of a crown—his interview with his officers at the termination of the war—his thoughts after retirement as expressed in a letter to Lafayette . . . his last words to Congress. . . . His behavior in the field and in council, and his dignified withdrawal to private life—are great. He could advance and he could withdraw."

At the time of Washington's death, Weems wrote triumphantly to Carey again: "I've something to whisper in your lug. Washington you know is gone! Millions are gasping to read something about him. I am nearly primed and cocked for 'em. Six months ago I set myself to collecting anecdotes of him. You know I live conveniently for that work. My plan! I give his history, sufficiently minute—I accompany him from the start, thro' the French & Indian & British or Revolutionary wars, to the Presidents chair, to the throne in the hearts of 5,000000 of people. I then show that his unparrelled [sic] rise and elevation were owing to his Great Virtues: 1. His Veneration for the diety *or* religious Principles, 2. His Patriotism, 3. His Magnanimity, 4. His Industry, 5. His Temperance

& Sobriety, 6. His Justice &c &c. Thus I hold up his great Virtues . . . to the imitation of our Youth.

"All this I have lined and enlivened with Anecdotes *apropos, interesting* and *entertaining.* I have read it to several Gentlemen whom I thought judges, such as a Presbyterian Clergyman, Classical Scholars &c, &c. and they all commend it much. . . . I read a part to one of my Parishioners, a first rate lady, and she wished I would print it promising to take one for each of her children (a bakers dozen)." The printing of the proposed work would not use more than three "royal sheets on long primer. We can sell it," he promised, "with great rapidity for 25 or 37 cents, and it would not cost 10. . . . I am thinking that you could vend it admirably; as it will be the first. I can send it on, half of it, immediately."

There is no evidence at all that Weems had had any personal acquaintance with Washington. Indeed, the latter may not have been at all pleased with the use to which Weems had put the casually appreciative notes that he had written upon receiving gift copies of Weems's edition of the *Sure and Certain Means of Abtaining a Long and Healthy Life* and *The Philanthropist.* And, though in March, 1799, he had written a polite reply to Weems's inquiry about the reliability of a person with whom Weems planned to do business, there seems to be no likelihood that the two ever met.

But sources of information were available to Weems. He did indeed "live conveniently for the work." The neighborhood abounded with people who had their own personal reminiscences of Washington, sometimes perhaps allowing imagination to supply what memory could not quite recover. The Rev. Lee Massey, who had served the old Pohick church when Washington attended it, had anecdotes to offer. And Weems drew freely from the popular *Short Sketch of Washington's Life and Character,* written by "a Gentleman of Maryland," which had been printed in London in 1780 to provide examples of courage to American prisoners of war then incarcerated in England.

It can also be suspected that *The Life and Memorable Actions of George Washington,* printed early in 1800 by George Keating of Baltimore, may have been, not a first version of Weems's pamphlet as most bibliographers suggest, but a source from which he drew almost to the point of plagiarism. Like his pamphlet, it was presented as "a pattern-book of imitation to the rising youth of America," and it contained several anecdotes identical to some that Weems would use. But it was a lacklustre production with little of the free-swinging rhetoric that identifies Weems's writing as surely his. Rather than being an early version of what he wrote, it seems likely to have been a principal source of much of his anecdotal material.

For *A History of the Life and Death, Virtues and Exploits of General George Washington,* with its dedication to Mrs. George Washington appropriately dated February 22, 1800, and signed as from "her sincere though unknown friend," is vintage Weems. What though Washington, "this truly great man . . . was the son by a second marriage, a circumstance," wrote Weems, "which it is hoped will effectually stop the mouths of those enemies of American population who are eternally bawling against *second* marriages. And it is likewise hoped," he continued, "that it will comfort the nerves of those chicken-livered batchelors, who are afraid to wed—afraid to wander in the Elysian fields of *matrimony,* lest they should encounter a group of their own angel-faced children. Timid mortals! Depopulation of your country! take courage and be happy!"

And with that Weems was off and away, down what by then were not unfamiliar paths. He knew to whom he wrote— simple people with just enough money in pocket to be tempted to buy an edifying small pamphlet. Washington's education, like theirs, he assured them, had been "of the private and proper sort. Dead languages, pride, and pedantry had no charms for him who always preferred sense to sound, the kernel to the shell. A grammatical knowledge of his mother tongue, the mathematics, geography, history, natural and moral philosophy, were the valuable objects of his youthful studies; and in these he made the proficiency of one who always loved to go deep."

Washington's early and "glorious ambition" was "to serve his country," and in that service he "was happier by far than the little souls . . . in Williamsburg fiddling and feasting in the Rawleigh tavern." And he was as resourceful as he was brave, brimful of native ingenuity. When he offered advice to General Braddock on how effectively to counter Indian attack, that worthy "swelled and reddened with unmanly rage. 'High times, by God!' he exclaimed strutting to and fro, with arms akimbo. 'High times! when a young Buckskin man teach a British General how to fight!'"

Washington was a person sent by God to save his people from slavery. He was "*the man* who for the greatest of all purposes had cheerfully relinquished every pleasure of life, and bravely exposed himself to all its evils, *the man* who for seven long years of difficulty and danger had manifested the most unflinching zeal for his country, and had been the honoured instrument of securing to them liberty, property, and every thing most dear and valuable—*the man*, who, in consequence of all this possessed so entirely the hearts of his army and of the nation, that he could easily have made himself their master.—They now saw this man scorning to abuse his power to the dishonour of his mother-country," but who, instead, bowed to the will of his countrymen, served them unswervingly well, and then "piously laying down his unbounded power," returned in retirement to humble occupations.

He was a religious man. "Do we not daily meet with melancholy instances of youth, lovely as innocence, sparkling as wit, and promising to the full of their parents wishes, who, yet merely for lack of religion make shipwreck of all their precious cargo; sacrificing their glory to grog; making conscience their curse, this life a purgatory, and the next a hell!! In fact, a man though of greatest talents without religion is but like a gorgeous ship without ballast: highly painted and with flowing canvas, she launches out upon the deep, and during a smooth sea and gentle breeze, she moves along stately as the pride of the ocean, but as the stormy winds descend, and the blackening billows begin to roll, suddenly she is overset and disappears forever."

And Washington was a person of deep-seated morality, unlike those of whom we "daily hear," said Weems, who are "by dice and cards, draining their fellow citizens to the last guinea, reducing them to a dunghill, or driving them to a pistol! Do we not hear of men of honour corrupting their neighbours wives and daughters, and then murdering their husbands in duels? Bind such selfish, such inhuman beings by a sense of honour!! Why not bind roaring Lions with a cobweb?"

Washington was not like that. Though a man among men, he was attentive to duty. One gentleman has assured me, testified Weems, "that dining one day at head-quarters in the company of a number of officers, he expected, as was very natural, to have had a free swig of some good drink, such as Porter, Punch, Wine, &c. but how did his palate fall on hearing the general cry out, 'come gentlemen here's a plenty of good whiskey and water, and water and whiskey; don't be bashful but call freely.' It was his habit, when 'his hour of duty was done,' to fill his glass and with a smile call out to his friends around the social board, 'Well, gentlemen, here is bon repos! and immediately withdraw to business.'"

Then Weems interjects a small comic anecdote about General Wayne, "who happily for America understood fighting better than French, had somehow or other taken up a notion that this same bon repos, to which Washington always made such conscience of giving his last bumper, must have been a great warrior in times of old." So one evening, having "by some extraordinary luck gotten hold of two or three dozen of good wine, he invited a parcel of fellow-officers to . . . help him break them to the cause of America."

Dinner over and the cloth removed, "the hero of Stony Point cried out *'come my brave fellows and fill your glasses, here's to old bon repose forever.'* " When the officers having drunk the toast, turned up their glasses, and started one and all to go, "Hey-day!" cried the General, "What's all this gentlemen, what's all this?" When the meaning of the phrase was explained to him, he burst out, "Well then damn bon repos and take your seats again, for by the Lord you shant leave till we have started every drop of every drink."

Weems was clumsy at comedy. He was better at exhortation and in providing homely examples of the goodness of virtue and the badness of vice. Washington was unashamedly a cultivator of the land, proud to put his hand to hoe, pruning hook, or plough. He worked hard in his fields and orchards, and manured them well, aiming at "teaching his countrymen the art of enriching their lands." He was a foe to idleness— and with that Weems was reminded of another moral tale. "What," he asked, "was it that harried poor Mr. A—— to that horrid act of suicide which froze the blood of all who heard it?" It was idleness, that bane of unthinking people. "Having *nothing* to *do*," this unfortunate man who had a young wife who "was all that we could conceive of sweetness, tenderness and truth in an Angel's form; and his three beauteous babes were the three graces in smiling infancy"—this unfortunate man "strolled to a tavern and to a card table, where he lost his all." Death was his only refuge.

But idleness was farther and more insidiously spread than in the experience of this unfortunate young man. It gripped a whole society. "What is the cause of all that horrid uproar which often throws our towns into such fear and trembling, on the evenings of our great holidays! Idleness. *Merciful heavens!* what wild tumultuous throng is that, on yonder *restless heaving* field? What clouds of dust! What swarming din of ten thousand discordant voices, *whooping* and *bellowing, cursing,* and *swearing.* Why surely the Devil's milleneum has begun, and all hell is turned out to celebrate the joyous occasion! No, it is no more than the rag-tag of a town, just escaped from the hand of *industry,* and got out there together with a sharkskin in pocket, drinking and roaring, racing and cock-fighting, betting and playing the D---l in a thousand shocking shapes."

For though Washington's career is briefly sketched, this little book is less concerned with that than, as its title had promised, with Washington's imitable virtues. Pages are devoted to his benevolence, his kindliness, and his sense of justice, the whole seasoned with moral interludes in which those virtues can be made to seem usable and available to all. Washington was a person who could not be bought. He refused pay for his military services—he was said to have turned down $70,000 offered to him. And apropos to this, Weems reminded his readers that "the famous British Minister, Sir Robert Walpole, used to say in open day that there was no man so honest but he might be bought if you would but bid boldly up to his price! How would he have dropped his Beef-steak if he had heard this anecdote of Washington."

For Washington was indeed a model, especially to youth: "Reader! Go thy way, think of Washington and HOPE. Though humble thy birth, low thy fortune, and few thy friends, still think of Washington and HOPE. Like him, honour thy God and delight in glorious toil. . . . Fed by the divine Oil of Religion, the flame of his virtue burned higher and higher." His life furnished "glorious proof of the infinite importance of religion."

The fool does not know this. "Religion's not for *his money, yet*. He choses rather to gratify his passions first. He shuffles and cuts one poor fellow out of a few hundreds—gives another a broken head—and cripples a third in a duel; or swallows fish, flesh and pastry till he puff again, and swills wine, toddy, and grog till he tumble under the table; or corrupts wife, widow, and maid that are fools enough to barter their honour and happiness for his *perjury* and pence.

"And having thus run on to the fag end of his cash, credit and constitution, blazing his way through society, by just the same marks that would follow the progress of a satyr or a devil, despised by the world, and with a hell of guilt and remorse in his own breast, he now thinks to quit scores with God and men—by turning infidel and crying up the 'Age of Reason'!! Pshaw! he was now safe and happy . . . now he has discovered, oh! glorious discovery that Jesus Christ is no better than an imposter, and that the bible is all a *mere lie*, invented by politicians and priests to frighten people *into* order, and *out* of their money."

The Parson was now filled with pulpit power as he reached his peroration. "Miserable man!" he thundered, "the slave and drudge of ever-craving, ever unsatisfied lusts of a vile body," who never knows "the exquisite and honourable pleasures of innocence, that innocence that would give you to lead the dignified life of a WASHINGTON on earth, to die his peaceful death, and shine a glorious angel with him for ever and ever in Heaven! . . . Let us follow Washington in the path of his virtue," learning by his example "that diligence and fair dealing are the surest steps to wealth. . . . While fools who think that Gambling and Knavery are nearer steps to wealth often die, like Rats, in prisons and poorhouses. . . . Guineas coined in the mint of iniquity have not the stamp of Washington upon them. . . . Let me entreat you, my fellow citizens . . . to imitate their greatest because the best example in his exemplary life."

89

Thus alternating between the language of the pulpit and the simpler language of fireside or tavern, he provided homely but horrific examples of what can happen when people stray from the God-directed ways exemplified in the life of Washington. The pamphlet ends with the retelling of a fable from AEsop in which the sun and wind contend in bringing comfort to people, a contest in which the heavenly sun is victor.

And the pamphlet did wondrously well. "I could sell thousands of them," said Weems, and he did. It was reprinted twice in its first year. Printers in Pennsylvania, New York, New Jersey, and Georgia brought out subsequent editions in rapid succession. People read it. Literary people, like a reviewer in Charles Brockden Brown's culturally ambitious *Monthly Magazine and American Review* in New York, found it a "whimsical production," filled with "as entertaining and edifying" material "as can be found in the annals of fanaticism and absurdity." But no matter! It did well.

Nothing is said in it about a cherry tree or young Washington's little hatchet, about the dream that Washington's mother had that forecast his tremendous success, or about his being discovered in prayer at Valley Forge. These would not be brought together until six years later, when in a fifth edition Weems worked toward expanding the pamphlet into a book.

But even in its early editions, his life of Washington catapulted him to instant fame. In January, 1802, at the invitation of the Governor of New Jersey, he delivered before the legislature of that state a spirited oration on *The Beauties and Beatitudes of a Republic* that was so well received that it was immediately printed, to become another pamphlet to be added to the increasing number of his own writings that he had for sale. Its theme was simple, and familiar: little children, let us love one another, for we have so much to be thankful for. A republic offered safety, wealth, prosperity, peace, and the pleasant exercise of increasing its population. Particularly satisfying to Weems on that occasion was that the "legislators, Old & Young, married and single" had purchased "to a man" more copies of *Hymen's Recruiting Serjeant* than of the Bible that he also presented for sale.

But then Weems was offered a dollar a day for expenses and a commission up to 25% for getting subscriptions for John Marshall's massive four-volumed official life of Washington, and he quit working for Mathew Carey. No more jolting over perilous roads in his little chaise. He was to be furnished with a light stage and "a pair of light-footed horses," so that now, he said, "I can travel with considerable dispatch." But his zeal for vending was to overtake him. He could not resist at the same time selling what he had left of Carey's stock, and his own books also. Thus serving three masters, he satisfied none.

He seems first to have extended his territory farther into the South during the early months of 1804, and what he saw there, especially in Charleston, tempted him "like a bird of passage to spend the winter in the South, and the autumn and summer months in the North," for during the summer months, "the Gentry of this Country," he observed, "are scattered abroad like sheep without a shepherd" and are "lean as so many rabbits in the Dog days, without a dollar to spend." But in the winter, "they are all in their towns thick as bees and merry as Crickets, with every man his pocket full of dollars from the sale of his Cotton bags & rice barrels."

But his first impressions of the deep South were not completely happy. "I live here at much cost & in much wretchedness, cut from the loveliest Wife & Fondest children on earth," he wrote from Savannah. And from Charleston, where he found "mosquitoes singing and gallinippers stinging," he complained that his "prospects as to *Comfort, Health, Life,* &c. are gloomy and unpromising—Even the natives are afraid to travel thro the Sultry, infected air of this fenny, loggy,

91

dreadful Country. Shou'd anything happen to me, I cherish hope," he told his new employer, "that you will do justice to my poor Widow & children."

But he dutifully returned, remaining there on one foray for almost a year, from the late spring of 1806 to the early winter of 1807, sorrowing then that he could not be with his wife when their second son was born. He fit better now into the lifestyles of Georgia and South Carolina. He was proud to discover that he was popular there, that his lectures on education, meant to sell his own books, were well attended and well received. He enjoyed rubbing elbows with the wealthy folk at Hilton Head. He even began to think of settling somewhere in the area permanently. And he gradually gave over his efforts to sell Marshall's cumbersome volumes and paid more attention to what he thought to be more easily vendible and more useful books.

No opportunity was let go by in keeping his assortment of wares before the public. Attached to an essay on "The Honest Lawyer," in the *Charleston Times* in July, 1806, that celebrated the life and achievements of the late George Wythe of Virginia, and in which he gave personal recollections of that gentleman which were said to have surprised and astonished some of Wythe's closer friends, he appended a notice that "Mason Locke Weems . . . has still a few red Morocco Family Bibles, with Cuts; Hymen's Recruiting Sergeant for poor Bachelors; the great Algernon Sydney for Politicians; and Montague on Fates and Fortunes of all the ancient republics, a very valuable book, just printed and beautifully bound, price One Dollar."

He had something for everyone. His lectures on education, particularly on the education of women, were announced, and sometimes printed in the newspapers of Savannah and Charleston, each with a fillip at the end calling attention to the books he had for sale. In "A Meditation for the Fourth of July" in the Savannah *Public Advertiser* in 1807, he pled for

Handbill, in Weems's handwriting,
offering Marshall's *Life of Washington* for sale.

an increasing bond of love among all people: "not he who *knows most* but he who *loves best* is the best republican," for "love with her graces and virtues" provides "the very ligatures of a republic," so that whoever "by *fraud* or *violence* sins against the law of love, is, so far forth, a traitor and a murderer of his country."

By 1807, he seems to have given over completely his attempts to sell subscriptions for Marshall's life of Washington, and was back again as an agent for Carey, somewhat chastened, but ready for another strenuous push at distributing more useful and more saleable books. "I am no longer," he wrote, "the credulous Romantic & therefore imprudent & unprosperous character that I formerly was." He grieved that with "education & capacity perhaps equal to the generality of money making Lawyers," he had "never made much owing to a lack of knowledge of men and business."

But he did know what books would sell. He was certain now that he could put together a life of Washington more suitable and more saleable than that contained in Marshall's large and cumbersome volumes. So he rewrote and expanded what he had written before into a sixth edition in 1808, in which the transformation from pamphlet to book became nearly complete. Weems now for the first time identified himself as having been the rector of Mount Vernon Parish, and the text of what has since been known, praised, or condemned, as "Weems's Washington" began to take final shape. A year later, he sold its copyright to Mathew Carey, and after that had little opportunity to tinker with its text.

Carey marketed it well, new editions appearing in rapid succession during Weems's lifetime, and an estimated twenty-some editions after that. Except for Franklin's *Autobiography*, it is perhaps the only book of its period that is still in print, and in several editions.

Like the pamphlet, it emphasized the private rather than the public character of Washington, "the bright ploughshare that he loved . . . his wheat crowned fields, waving in yellow ridges before the wanton breeze . . . his hills whitened over with flocks—or his clover-covered pastures spread with innumerable herds—or his heat-clad servants, with songs rolling the heavy harvest before them." These satisfied the hero now.

Where but in America, "this vast continent where the Almighty has reared his cloud-capt mountains, and spread his sea-like lakes, and poured his mighty rivers, and hurled down his thundering cataracts," could such wonders exist, "so far superior to any thing of the kind in other continents."

The purple mountain majesties, the fruited plains! And these crowned with brotherhood, for every young American "may become a Washington in piety and patriotism—in industry and honour." For certainly, "great men and great deeds are designed for America."

Walt Whitman, who would sing his country's expansive possibilities, was not yet born. Ralph Waldo Emerson, who would counsel recognition within each person of unique possibilities for service, was a toddler in Boston. But Weems was suggesting ideas that they would make plain. Not many years later, Abraham Lincoln would read his words in a log house on the American frontier, and would be inspired by them.

For Weems's voice was the secret and unspoken voice of many of his countrymen. City-bred or university-trained people composed but a small part of his audience. His importance is that he spoke and continued to speak to honest, god-fearing working people in language fitted to their understanding and eliciting their sympathetic response.

He explained to them how Washington "in the days of his youth, when his feet were swift toward the nests of birds; or, when wearied in the chace of the butterfly, he laid him down on his grassy couch and slept, while ministering spirits with their roseate wings, fanned his glowing cheeks, and kissed his lips of innocence." He told them of young Washington's "little pug nose to smell the sweet flowers! and pretty ears to har the sweet sound! and a lovely mouth for his bread and butter! and O, the little teeth to cut it for him! and the dear little tongue to prattle with!" It was the boy Washington's father who was said thus to have described his son. As a father himself, Weems was certainly capable of inventing terms of parental admiration and placing them without shame into another father's mouth. He never heard these words, but if he had been there, he might have. And to doting young parents their appeal was certainly certain.

Even as a boy, Washington began to fit himself for the rigors of soldiering. "At jumping with the long pole, or heaving heavy weights . . . he scarcely had an equal. And as to running, the swift-footed Achilles could hardly have matched his speed." One boyhood friend remembered that he had "often seen him throw a stone across the Rappahannock, at the lower ferry of Fredericksburg." He thought nothing of holding a heavy shotgun "at arms-length, and blazing away at the swans on the Potomac, of which he has been known to kill rank and file seven or eight at a shot."

These things were not invented by Weems, only embroidered by him in the telling. He wrote of what he had been told by people who had known Washington. Among them were a "very aged gentleman, formerly a schoolmate," John Fitzhugh, Esq., "who knew him well," Colonel Ben Temple, of King William County, "who was one of his aids in the French and Indian wars," an unnamed but "excellent old lady of Fredericksburg," Mr. Peake, "a sensible, honest manager of one of Washington's plantations," and "Mr. Lund Washington, long a manager of his Mount Vernon estate." Not least among them was an amiable "aged lady, who is a distant cousin" of Washington, "and when a girl spent much of her time in the family," who told him the story of the hatchet and the cherry tree.

Because that story has been so often told, and in so many

versions, it is here reproduced just as Weems finally presented it. Note that it is a hatchet, not a little hatchet that does damage to the tree—though in an earlier version, Weems had used the adjective which, despite his later deletion, clings to the hatchet in many later versions put together by people as unashamed as he in making a pretty story prettier. Note also that the cherry tree is not cut down as in many later retellings: it is barked, bruised, and apparently died overnight. Nor does George stand beside the tree confronted by his father. The confession takes place within the house. This then is the story as the amiable aged lady is quoted as telling it:

"When George," said she, "was about six years old, he was made the wealthy master of a *hatchet!* of which, like most little boys, he was immoderately fond, and was constantly going about chopping every thing that came in his way. One day, in the garden, where he often amused himself hacking his mother's pea-sticks, he unluckily tried the edge of his hatchet on the body of a beautiful young English cherry-tree, which he barked so terribly, that I don't believe the tree ever got the better of it. The next morning the old gentleman finding out what had befallen his tree, which, by the by, was a great favourite, came into the house, and with much warmth asked for the mischievous author, declaring at the same time, that he would not have taken five guineas for his tree. Nobody could tell him anything about it. Presently George and his hatchet made their appearance. *George,* said his father, *do you know who killed that beautiful little cherry-tree yonder in the garden?* This was a *tough question;* and George staggered under it for a moment; but quickly recovered himself: and looking at his father, with the sweet face of youth brightened with the inexpressible charm of all-conquering truth, he bravely cried out, '*I can't tell a lie, Pa; you know I can't tell a lie. I did cut it with my hatchet.*'—*Run to my arms, you dearest boy,* cried his father in transports, *run to my arms; glad am I, George, that you killed my tree; for you have*

97

paid me for it a thousand fold. Such an act of heroism in my son, is more worth than a thousand trees, though blossomed with silver, and their fruits of purest gold."

Washington's activities as soldier are sketched much as they had been in the earlier versions. The story of General Braddock exploding in indignation that a "young Buckskin" should dare to "teach a British General how to fight" is repeated almost verbatim. Much of the expansion from pamphlet to book was managed by extended descriptions of scene or action. Frontier lands were "gloomy haunts of ravening beasts and of murderous savages" where "no voices ever broke the awful silence . . . save the hiss of rattlesnakes, the shrieks of panthers, the howls of Indians, and howling tempests." British troops rushing in retreat are like "some tremendous whirlwind, whose roaring sweep all at once darkens the day, riding the air in tempest, so sudden and terrible, amidst clouds of dust, and smoke and flame."

Weems liked extended Homeric metaphors. Washington, gentle in peace, in battle was like "the big lion of Zara, calling his brindled sons to battle against the mighty rhinoceros, if he mark their falling manes and crouching to his side, instantly puts on all his terrors—his eyes roll in blood—he shakes the forest with his deepening roar, till, kindled by their father's fire, the maddening cubs swell with answering rage, and spring undaunted on the Monster. Thus stately and terrible rode *Columbia's first and greatest son,* along the front of his halted troops. The eager wish for battle flushed over his burning face, as, rising on his stirrups, he waved his sword towards the hostile camp."

And enemy forces in retreat? That was, said Weems, "As when a mammoth suddenly dashes in among a thousand buffaloes, feeding at large on the vast plains of Missouri; all at once the innumerous herd, with wildly rolling eyes, and hideous bellowings, break forth into flight, while close at their heels, the roaring monster follows—earth trembles as they fly. Such was the noise in the chase of Tarleton, when the swords of Washington's cavalry pursued his troops from Cowpen's famous fields. It was like a peal of thunder, loud roaring at first, but gradually dying on the ear as it rolls away along the distant air."

Some readers may have scratched their heads over the precise meaning of such verbal pyrotechnics. But, my, they did sound nice. It set a mind to soaring.

Most readers could certainly follow him more surely when he explained to them that the switcell that dauntless Bostonians drank to quiet their nerves was only "a mild moralizing malmsy, made of molasses and sugar, which the prudent Yankees drink to the great benefit of their health and senses, while their southern neighbours are be-fooling and be-poisoning themselves with grog."

And a familiar voice is recognized when he reminds them that at the Battle of Monmouth, many combatants "died of the extreme *heat*, and by drinking *cold* water."

Washington's true benevolence is underscored when he is remembered as having turned captive Hessian mercenaries over to Dutch settlers who invited them to settle, as they had, in this land of so much promise. "Our lands are rich," they said, "come help in cultivating them. Our tables are covered with fat meats, and with milk and honey; come set down and eat with us like brothers. Our daughters are young and beautiful and good; then shew yourselves *worthy*, and you shall have our daughters, and we will give you of our land and cattle, that you may work and grow rich and happy as we are."

For America was indeed a land of promise, "where the poorest Lazarus may get his *fifty cents* a day for the commonest labour," even at "the healthy and glorious labours of the plough," and where he can "buy the daintiest bread of corn flour at a *cent a pound*. "Why then," he asked, "is any man hungry, or thirsty, or naked, or in prison." Herring from the Potomac, "the finest herrings in the world . . . when salted, furnish not only to the wealthy a charming relish to their tea and coffee, but also to the poor a delicious substitute for bacon."

The only people who suffer in America are those whose parents have brought them up in "sloth, pleasure, and dress, as young noblemen, and then leave them without estate, profession or trades, to turn gamblers, sharpers or horse thieves."

How different, how excellent was Washington—his benevolence, industry, and patriotism, and his legacy to his people in his farewell address. How terrible the possibility of disunion among the people whom he had led to freedom. People divided must fall.

As he had in *The Philanthropist*, Weems pled again for amity among all Americans. He was reminded that "even the piney woods of Georgia and South Carolina, strewed with mangled carcasses . . . give awful proof, that when brethren turn their swords into each other's bowels, war degenerates into murder, and battles into butchers." He reminded readers how "in the last war, between whigs and tories of the southern states," men had "been dragged out of their houses, and, amidst the screams of their wives and children have been hung up to trees, or cut to pieces with swords with the most savage joy . . . their houses burnt, their cattle and slaves carried off, and their widows and children out, crying, and without bread, into the barren woods."

He urged them then to take to heart the words and the character of Washington and to "rise up with joy to co-operate with God in the glorious work of beautifying, with the fruits of righteousness, this goodly land."

Then, the homily disguised as biography ends, as all fine sermons must, with a benediction, as Weems petitions that his countrymen be taught to "entertain a brotherly affection and love for one another . . . to do justice, to love mercy," and be endowed "with that charity, humility, and pacific temper of mind which were the characteristics of the divine author of our blessed religion."

The book is a potpourri, with something for everyone. No wonder it sold, and kept on selling. "I could maintain my family handsomely on that single book," said Weems, and he more than once wished that he could buy back its copyright again. Hugh Henry Brackenridge, whose fictionized satire of native politics, *Modern Chivalry,* was just then appearing in volume after volume, found Weems's book judiciously to blend the pathetic with the comic, and to contain much good sense. But the austere *Monthly Anthology* in Boston dismissed it as "a specimen of writing which for variety and oddity is almost unique in the annals of literature. With a style of rotundity and bombast . . . he has intermingled the ludicrous quaintness of Joe Miller, and he often transports us from a trail of religious moralizing, more than commonly exalted, to the low cant and balderdash of the ranks and drinking table." Perhaps, said the New England reviewer, it should "be termed a novel founded on fact."

The Life of George Washington was a moral tale, an exemplum, one of the oldest of literary forms, meant to entertain in order to instruct and correct. Weems certainly had done that as well as any New Englander had yet done.

7. LIVES OF GREAT MEN

"High, Low, Jack and the Game"

T he *Life of George Washington* doing so well, Weems was tempted to try his hand at biography again. In Georgetown, South Carolina, he had met General Peter Horry, who had been a friend and military companion of the late General Francis Marion, the "swamp fox," whose daring exploits during the American Revolution in harassing British forces by swift surprise attacks had contributed much to the ending of hostilities in South Carolina. Marion represented the common man, the man whose chief talents were bravery, ingenuity, and loyalty. He was the kind of person in whom Americans of all ranks could take pride. He invited emulation.

Horry had letters and documents pertaining to his friend's career, and had apparently also roughed out a history of Marion's life and exploits. But Horry was not a literary person. He was a bluff and hearty old soldier with many memories, and he was eager that the exploits of his former comrade should not be forgotten. So, early in 1808, he turned his materials over to Weems for editing and publication.

And Weems went right to work. "I beg you to indulge in no fears," he wrote Horry, "that Marion will ever die, while I can say or write anything to immortalize him." He thought that he could get the work done quickly: "I hope in three weeks to have it all chiseled out in the rough cast." Then it "will take me about three weeks to polish and colour it in a style that will, I hope, sometimes excite a smile, and sometimes bring forth a tear."

But he overestimated himself. Other things got in the way.

There were the usual, or perhaps by now the unusual, parish duties. There was great busyness in seeing to the expanded version of the Washington biography, and more busyness still in transferring its copyright to Mathew Carey. Besides, there was his bookselling route, which had him toiling, he said, from door to door, *"walking, talking, pleading & preaching to the Multitudes,"* until he had become "an Alien to my family, a wanderer on the earth, oftimes cold, wet, dinnerless & weary."

Not least was the begetting of two sons named Marion, the first living hardly more than six weeks, and the second born just three days before Weems was finally able to inform Horry, on December 13, 1809, more than eighteen months since the project was begun, that "the history of the great Marion . . . is finished."

He had written it, he said, "in my own way, and knowing the passion of the times for novels, I have endeavoured to throw your ideas and facts . . . into the garb and dress of a military romance." He hoped, he said, that what he had done would not offend Horry's delicacy.

But it did, and greatly. "I gave you leave," said the old General, "to embellish the work,—but entertained not the least idea of what has happened. . . . You have carved and mutilated it with so many erroneous statements, that your embellishments, observations and remarks must necessarily be erroneous as proceeding from false grounds. Most certainly 'tis not my history but your romance. . . . Can you suppose I can be pleased," he continued, "with reading particulars (though ever so elevated by you) of Marion and myself, when I know such never existed?"

Horry was correct. Weems had taken liberties indeed, and he had written the book in the first person, as if Horry was telling it, and had put the old soldier's name on the title page. But Horry was also wrong when he insisted that if the book had been written as "a history of real performance," it "would always be read with pleasure," but that now, "as a fictitious invention of the brain, once read would suffice."

For *The Life of Gen. Francis Marion, A Celebrated Partisan Officer, in the Revolutionary War* may well be Weems's most successful book, though not in sales perhaps, in which respect the biography of Washington and *Hymen's Recruiting Serjeant* undoubtedly did better, though Weems, perhaps in authorial euphoria, more than once insisted that it did quite as well as either. It was written with great gusto and greater inventiveness, a romance indeed, and military also.

It was written as the biography of Washington had been written, as a book to inspire young people, and to interest their elders. And it was written in a brisk but homely colloquial style, with few of the full-throated darts toward eloquence found in the biography of Washington. For all of its errors in fact or interpretation, it was alive with "the fantastic ardour of Weems" that did much, Carl Van Doren has testified, toward securing for Marion a firm place in history as the Agamemnon of the American Revolution.

Weems called him—or, rather, had Horry call him—the Washington of the South, and found it significant that both heroes had been born in the same year, both had early lost a father, both had served in Indian wars, both were heroes of the Revolution, and both, when their duties toward their country were done, retired to a life of quiet rural labor.

But there was a difference. Washington had been presented as a sturdy, strong person, larger than life, and capable of almost superhuman feats of strength and agility. Marion was a small man who became successful in spite of that. "I have it on good authority," wrote Weems, "that Marion, this great soldier, at his birth, was not larger than a New England lobster, and might easily enough have been put into a quart pot." If he had been born among "the Mohawks of Sparta," he would have been considered useless and "thrown into the horse pond with as little ceremony as a blind puppy."

At the age of twelve, to improve his health, his parents put him on board a little schooner bound for the West Indies. But the vessel was attacked by "some monstrous fish, probably a horn-back whale, who gave it such a terrible strike with its tail as started a plank." Captain, crew, and passenger quit the sinking ship in "a little jolly boat" and drifted helpless, scorched by the sun and with no provision in food or drink to sustain them. They devoured the flesh and drank the blood of a little dog that swam toward their boat, but that did rather more harm than good.

"About the tenth day the captain and mate leaped overboard raving mad, the day following, the two remaining seamen expired in the bottom of the boat." Finally rescued by a passing vessel, the boy was nursed back to health "by means of chocolate and turtle broth, sparingly given," and, though small, he was never puny again.

His was a tight-drawn, wiry strength. Never a handsome man, he was nonetheless admired for "cleanliness of person, neatness of dress, and gentlemanly manners." But for all of that, he was only a "swarthy, French phizzed Carolinian," an uncommon "smoke-dried" little man, whom simple, ordinary people could understand and emulate. For Marion set himself in no way above his fellows. But he was brave and resourceful, fearless in battle, and forgiving of his enemies when the battle was over. Like Washington, he set an example for young people to follow. What he had done, each of them, in their own ways, could do.

One of the features of the book was its praise of simple people, who were brave and honest, loved God, and settled happily into the place allowed them. Valiant Sergeant Jasper was a "youthful Sampson," who, when offered a commission, refused it, for, he said, "If I were to get a commission I would be forced to keep higher company; and then, as I don't know how to read, I should only be throwing myself in the way to be laughed at." The lesson was two-pronged, but simple. It spoke to young people about recognizing their limitations, and it spoke also about the necessity for education if one was to get ahead. And it spoke also to parents "who can waste on grog and tobacco that precious money" they "ought to educate their children with."

Weems knew his audience, and he knew his duty toward that audience also. He seasoned the book with vignettes of ordinary people who were as worthy of as much respect and admiration as were the men who led them—people like Captain Snipes of uncommon strength and courage, old Mrs. Jenkins and her unheralded heroism, Colonel Harry Lee's spunky little bugle boy, stout Sheriff John Wiley, and the pious but patriotic and martial Quaker, Peter Yarnall. He spoke of the loyalty of black Cudjo to his soldier master, recalling the times they had "wrestled and slept side by side" or "set out in full march to some favorite fruit-tree, or some cooling pond."

Sometimes he rose toward rhetorical heights, as when he pictured the doughty Scotch Sergeant McDonald, fierce in battle: "with his wide spread nostrils, and long extended neck, and glaring eye balls, he seemed as a flying dragon in search of prey." Brandishing his claymore, and "rising in his stirrups with high lift of arms he waved it three times in fiery circle over his head. . . . Then with a voice of thunder, he poured his *charging shout,* dreadful as the roar of a lion when close to his game . . . makes the last spring on the fat buffalo of his chase."

Less often than in the biography of Washington did his rhetoric run away with him. He now used simpler language, of a kind familiar to country readers. Marion's soldiers, though a rag-tail lot "who could no more pass by a keg of brandy, than a young monkey could pass a basket of apples," were pictured "rubbing their horses, like young men preparing for a ball or barbecue," or, at another time were spoken of as sleeping "snug as fleas in a sheep skin." Abandoning the sometimes inflated rhetoric of the earlier biography, he now used homely comparisons of a kind familiar to country readers.

When an early British attempt to take Charleston failed and the hardy American militia men were rewarded with "a couple of fat beeves and a hogshead of rum" to refresh them after "a hard day's work," and when the gentlemen of Charleston accompanied by their ladies came from the city to congratulate them, the weary soldiers put on their "best bibs and tuckers to honor their coming. 'Freedom's sons are we,' they shouted, 'and d--n the villains that would make us slaves.'"

War was dreadful. It was "that *sunshine and barking time* of rogues which calls them out, thick as may-day sun calls out the rattle snakes from their stony crannies." Amid the disruptions of war, "thieves turn out in shoals: and devils, like hungry fishing-hawks" scream for their prey. Fields are laid fallow, the "sacred plough was every where seen rusting—Grog shops and Nanny houses were springing up as thick as hops—and the house of God saw nobody—but if there were a devil's house (a dram shop) close by you might be sure to see *that* crowded with poor Lazarites with red noses and black eyes, and the fences all strung along with starved tackies in grapevine bridles and sheep skin saddles."

But Marion, though hating war, ennobled it. When he and Horry went "vagrant hunting," rounding up men in grog shop and tavern for their rag-tail army, "I hardly think," Horry was quoted as saying, that "we could in the same time have caught as many racoons in any swamp" on the Pee Dee River. The British were "a handful of hawks; the poor Carolinians a swarm of rice-birds, and rather than be plucked to the pin-feather or plucked to the bone," they joined or were pressed into service with Marion's small guerilla band. But sometimes the embattled people "were fane to flatter these furious falcons, and oftimes to chirp and sing when they were much in the humor to hate and curse."

The British were invading Turks, ready, they were said to have said, to make Charleston "our Constantinople! and our Circassa, this sweet Carolina famed for beauties! 'Prepare the baths,' they shouted, 'the perfumes and the spices! bring forth the victim and the rose buds! and tap the old Madiera, that our souls may all be joy!' "

And it was Marion, that "swarthy French phizzed Carolinian," who "with only thirty of his ragged countrymen, issuing out of the swamp," who "dared to turn his horse's head toward this all conquering foe. He hit them *hip and thigh* again and again . . . slipping through a briar patch with the facility of a weasel through the chinks of a chicken-coop."

Drinking was a bane among Carolinians, but especially among the British, a cause certainly of their eventual defeat. Weems presented many a moral tale about that, the first being of two unfortunate officers who, pleased with British successes in bombarding the fort at Charleston, said, one to the other, " 'Well, d--n my eyes Frank, the play is over! so lets go below and hob nob to a glass of wine, for I'm devilish dry.'

" 'With all my heart, Jack,' replied the other; so down they whipped into the cabin, where wine and glasses had been standing all day upon the table. At that moment," wrote Weems, "one of our two and forty pounders being just loaded, Marion called to colonel Moultrie, and asked if it would not be well 'to give them a *last blow*.' 'Yes,' replied Moultrie, 'give them the *parting kick*.'

"Marion clapped the match, and away in thunder and lightning went the ball, which entering the cabin window shattered the two friends; thence raging through the bulkheads and steerage, it shivered three sailors on the main deck, and after all, bursting through the forecastle into the sea, sank with a sullen joy to the bottom."

British officers "from early life . . . discovered a total dislike to the ennobling pleasures of literature and devotion, but a boundless passion for the brutalizing sports of the bear-garden and cock-pit. Bull-baiters, cock-fighters, and dog-worriers turned officers, they had no idea of conquering Americans but by cutting their throats or knocking out their brains." Weems even mentions the villainy of one Major Weymiss, who just may have been, though distantly, a kinsman, who was "by birthright a Scotsman, but in principle and practice a Mohawk," and who led a band of "lazy, dram-drinking, plunder-loving Tories" through the countryside, an evil man, notorious for perfidy.

And gambling also led people toward perdition. A band of Tory partisans sought to seek out and destroy Marion and his men. But the swamp fox was too much for them. While they drank and played at cards, he swooped down upon them. "Even their fiddles and fiddle bows and playing cards were strewed about their fires. One of the gamblers," said Weems, "though shot full dead, still held the cards hard gripped in his hands."

Then, showing perhaps more familiarity with card playing than might be expected of a clergyman, he continued by having Horry say, "Led by curiosity to inspect this sight, a dead gambler, we found that the cards he held were ace, duece, and jack. Clubs were trump. Holding high, low, and jack and the game in his hand, he seemed in a fair way to do well, but Marion came down on him with a trump, that spoiled his sport and non-suited him forever." The puns were dreadful, and the story old, but it was suited to Weems's purpose and must certainly have tempted a smile from his country readers.

But Marion himself was guilty of no such failings as cards

or drink. "I know of no religion," he is said to have said, "except of hearty love of God and man." Terrible in battle, he was nevertheless a man of peace. "Though he taught us," Horry was made to say, "to sleep in the swamps, to feed on roots, to drink the turbid waters of the ditch, to prowl nightly around the encampment of the foe, like lions round the habitations of the shepherds who had slaughtered their cubs," he was a man who sorrowed that it was man's "sad destiny . . . to kill one another."

He was the incorruptible man. Dining one day "with a squad of choice Whigs . . . he was so frequently pressed with bumpers of old wine that he thought himself in a fair way to get drunk. 'Twas in vain that he attempted to beat a retreat. His company swore, that that would never do for gen'l Marion. Finding, at last that there was no other way of escaping a debauch but by jumping out of the windows of the dining room, which was on the second story, he bravely undertook it. It cost him however an ankle. When the story got about Charleston, most people thought him to have been a great fool for his pains; but the event proved that Marion was right, and there is no policy like sticking to a moral duty." For when the British gathered to invade Charleston, Marion, unable to participate in its defense, was carried from the city on a litter, and was thus "providentially . . . preserved to his country when Charleston fell, as it soon did, with all our patriot troops."

Throughout Weems supplied more salutary anecdotes and moral admonition than he did biography. The lives of great men were in his view reminders to readers that they too might make their lives, if not sublime, at least honest, and decent. Even what Marion did, and when he did it, seemed unimportant. The book was made to instruct and to sell, and it apparently did both. It was "met everywhere," Weems insisted to Horry, "with unbounded applause."

When he sent a copy of its sixth edition to President James

Madison, he explained that the book "made a great noise in the country," and then barefacedly suggested, "If you shou'd be pleased with the Spirit of Marion, and think it ought to be universal among the youth of our Republic, you will do both them & me a great kindness by giving us a line commendatory of Marion as a schoolbook. My Life of Washington written for that purpose is now in its 21st edition; and from the demand for Marion I have reason to think that he will not be far behind." Madison replied that he had been greatly pleased with the vein of patriotism running through the book, as well as "the vivid pictures and fine moral lessons, for which the cause of your justly admired hero furnished you the happy occasions." That made Weems happy, and helped sell more books.

As in most of his literary judgments, Madison was correct. As a school book, an exemplar, *The Life of Gen. Francis Marion* deserved to do well. It instructed and sold. What more could be wanted of a book? The South Carolina novelist William Gilmore Simms, who would later write about Marion, testified that the "liberties that Weems took with Horry's documents did not, in all probability, except in one or two instances, affect the substantial history. He simply exercised the privilege of the old Historians. He put speeches into the mouths of his heroes. He gave us long dialogues, in which he furnished, pro and con, the eloquence, the patriotism, and the sentiment of his interlocutors. And this deceived nobody . . . for it so happened that his parties thus furnished with speech invariably talked like Weems himself." Using whatever material came to hand or mind, he did produce, in the words of his first biographer, "an unusually attractive historical romance."

This was not true of *The Life of Benjamin Franklin*, which appeared in 1815. This was almost completely a cut-and-paste performance. Its first section contains a reprinting of Franklin's *Autobiography*, carrying the story of his life until

111

1731. This is followed by a lackluster account of the rest of his life, so calmly straightforward that there is great suspicion that Weems had no hand in it, only scissors to clip from some unidentified source additional materials that the *Autobiography* had not revealed. Then the volume is beefed up with more than twenty essays and observations culled from Franklin's prose writings. But it did well. And every one of its several editions was identified as by M. L. Weems.

Late in life, in 1822, he put together a fourth biography, this time of William Penn. It is, almost throughout, a fictionized account, with Penn and his family, his adversaries, and friends in lively conversation, one with the other. It was "pleasing to learn" that Penn's father had "married early," as all good men should, and that "a dove-like spirit of meekness" had descended on "honest broad-brim'd William Penn" largely through the influence of his mother in whose "fond arms he found his dearest cradle, and his sweetest pillow on her snowy orbs."

Unlike the ignorant mother, she did not say to her son, "learn your books and you shall be a great man by and by." That would mean "nothing beyond a showy, college education, which though it may increase his pride and arrogance, seldom adds any thing to his divine and social affections, which alone makes a Young man amiable and happy." By being a great man she did not mean "only a great scholar; a great physician; a great lawyer; making a great deal of money; building great houses and so on—and after all, the dupe of his passions, and as miserable as pride, envy, hate, intemperance, and duelling can make him."

This, again, is vintage Weems. Many of the early chapters tell of the mother's pious conversations with her son, from the time that he is "a fine, plump, fleshy body of five or six," through his school days and his college years when he is expelled for having espoused Quakerism: "Like the Parent Eagle calling her young to his native skies, when she sees the breaking forth of the sun over all his golden clouds, thus did the tender mother . . . sow the seeds of religion in the soul of her son."

It was a religion of simple devoutness, without "cold read prayers; cold read sermons; noisy organs, with crowds of gay ones and great, professing to worship God, but evidently idolizing themselves and one another." Weems had by now put aside the rituals of divine service and the kind of religion that found, "both among the priests and their people a constant vieing with each other" over "who shall have the finest clothes and the most dazzling equipage." However "the great ones of the world . . . might look for pomp and parade, yet to the Almighty all this was an abomination of that approach to the soul . . . in a meek and docile spirit of a child."

The Life of William Penn represents what was apparently to be its author's final testimony on the place and importance of religion. It was religion democratized, and equally accessible to all. And its fount was the Christian Bible.

The Bible was enough. Weems was not the first, nor would he be the last, to tell the story of the "giddy and dissipated" young man who was converted to Christianity when a Bible that his mother had placed, unbeknownst to him, in his breast pocket diverted a bullet that would have pierced his heart. Then, "for the first time in his life, he fell on his knees and adored God."

But perhaps the Bible was not enough. Not long before this Weems had written to Mathew Carey that he contemplated "a noble addition to the Bible" which would set before the people of America the "brightness and blessings" of democracy—a kind of appendix, bringing divine scripture up to date. "I have got a synopsis nearly ready," he said. But either Carey, the good Roman Catholic, demurred or other projects which skimmed through the itinerate parson's head got in the way. The improved and democratic Bible seems not to have appeared.

113

The Life of William Penn ends with a fine, full account of Penn's treaty with and oration to the Indians, whom he considered not as savages but as brothers who, like him, sought only peace and contentment. Included is a listing of what he gave them in payment for their lands—how many hands of tobacco, fathoms of wampum, gallons of molasses, pounds of powder, jews harps, guns, and blankets. The volume is then fattened out with tributes to Penn by, among others, Edmund Burke and the Baron de Montesquieu, and with a collection of "Reflections and Maxims of William Penn," more than eight hundred of them, on such subjects as ignorance, education, tolerance, and charity.

"I do not see how Christians can possibly separate from one another," Weems had the Quaker leader say. "The lambs of God's fold never separate, though they may differ in the colours of their fleeces, some white and some black, yet still being all the same in innocence and gentleness, they do not separate, but cleave to one another. For what is it . . . that makes real Christians cleave to one another . . . but *perfect love* out of a PURE HEART, and how can those who possess it in themselves, but be charmed in others with that blessed spirit which is to do away with all fraud and violence from the earth, and fill it with all the precious fruits of universal righteousness."

And this, unless it can be proved otherwise, represented the openhearted good will of Parson Weems.

8. HOGARTH VERBALIZED

"Who Ever Heard of a Gambler Dying Rich"

eems had been peddling for Mathew Carey hardly more than a year, when in December, 1796, he came upon the engravings of William Hogarth, which he found to be of "the highest moral tendency." Hogarth's "pictur'd Morals," his vividly drawn portrayals of the evils and consequences of careless living, had been for years the rage in London and on the Continent. Why should they not, thought Weems, do as well among his customers? One picture indeed might be worth a thousand words. Weems wished that Carey would undertake to publish some of them: *The Harlot's Progress, Marriage a la Mode, The Idle Apprentice, The Four Stages of Cruelty,* and others, thirty-seven plates in all.

Done handsomely, he had no doubt that they would "greatly benefit the Public" and amply repay "the virtuous and truly patriotic toils of Carey & Weems." They would be expensive, to be sure, perhaps 20 guineas or $100 a volume, but, said Weems, "I have a notion that 2000 subscriptions might be procur^d." He had already spoken to some gentlemen in Virginia "who have all expressed an eagerness to have them." And other gentlemen in Maryland to whom he had spoken had "highly approv'd and instantly offered to patronize it."

The project seems to have been quite too costly to tempt the more cautious Carey. Weems, however, had also heard of, though perhaps had not seen, a volume of *Hogarth Moralized* done by an English clergyman some twenty years before. Might they not reproduce that, with a few of Hogarth's plates? Carey did not rise to that bait, but Weems still thought that "Hogarth's portraitures of Folly," though expensive, "would assuredly succeed in this country," by which he meant the American South, "as powerful incentives to the Correction of Morals," and they might add, he suggested to Carey, "another leaf to the evergreen Chaplet that already entwines your brows."

Though Carey could not be tempted, Weems was; so he began to compose and publish a series of Hogarthian prose pictures of the evils of murder, gambling, drunkenness, adultery, duelling, and unwifely conduct. The first is said to have appeared in 1801, close on the heels of his splurge of remedial recipes for happy marriages, pacific political conduct, and holding high the example of Washington to the youth of America. But no copy of *God's Revenge against Murder* has been found before 1807, when it ushered in a series of exemplary small tracts that during Weems's lifetime were surpassed only by his life of Washington and *Hymen's Recruiting Serjeant* in popular appeal, edition after edition appearing, paperbacked in plain grey wrappers, most of them selling, and selling fast at twenty-five cents each.

Popular fiction had not yet become fiction as it is known today. Tales were pretended not to have been invented. They were presented and verified as extracts from life, and they pointed inexorably to truths or warned of the monstrous effects of immorality. This was especially true in America, which had no Walter Scott to romanticize its history, no Laurence Sterne wittily to expose its idiosyncratic ways, nor a Henry Fielding to tell lusty tales of doing what comes naturally. Its model was Samuel Richardson, the pious English storyteller, and his successors and imitators who presented portentous warnings of what happens to people who behave in ways they should not.

Among Weems's prominent native contemporaries, Hugh

Henry Brackenridge, who liked what Weems as biographer had produced, wrote fiction as satire of the politics of the new country, and Charles Brockden Brown, his pen dipped in inherited moral requirements, tried valiantly to produce novels that, aside from instruction, had independent cause for being. But these were exceptions.

People wanted to be instructed as they read, and not in subtle ways, but by well-aimed blasts at what happens to people who do not behave in accordance with imposed standards. Life in the new country was very real and very earnest. Made-up stories were somehow immoral. There was so much else to do in shoring up the flimsy fabric of the young republic. But as for slices of life, in which virtue was rewarded, these could be devoured with lip-smacking appreciation or shivery apprehension.

That was the kind of thing that Weems learned to do explicitly well. His portraits of people snared by vice and suffering its consequences were sandwiched between rich slabs of explicit moral instruction. He took care that none mistook his meaning, by patiently and repetitiously explaining how the sad and thoughtless experiences of the people of whom he wrote might have been avoided had they enjoyed the glad experience of true Christian nurture and had they been offered opportunity to read books such as he had for sale.

God's Revenge against Murder seems to have been founded on fact, and Weems seems to have become victim of some recriminatory invective for having written it. But that only made it sell faster. It was presented to readers as "a tragedy, as lately performed, with unbounded applause (of the Devil and his court) by Ned Findley, Esq, one of the grand company of tragedians in the service of the Black Prince, who was so highly gratified with Mr. Findley's performance that he instantly provided him rooms in one of his own palaces; created him a knight of the most ignoble order of the halter; clapped bracelets on his wrists, and as an ornament around his neck, and in a few days promoted him to the ridge pole of the gallows in Edgefield court-house, South Carolina."

But the story centered on Mary, or Polly Middleton, also of the Edgefield district, who was barbarously mistreated at home by an unpleasant stepmother, "kept under hatches like a servant," her "spirits cowed." For refuge, Polly retreated to the home of an older sister. Comforted there by a handsome young man, a relative of her sister's husband, she unwisely submitted herself to his advances, and became pregnant. A "lamb that had wandered," she was turned from her sister's door and found her way back to her father's house where, the wicked stepmother having died, a new and kindly new stepmother, her father's fourth wife, briefly befriended her.

But her father, discovering that this good Mrs. Middleton had taken her in and comforted her, ordered that Polly be turned out again, taken by a slave and left with her baby on the highroad to Charleston. She discovered nearby a little cabin, and there she lived with her son, much as Nathaniel Hawthorne's Hester Prynne was to live with her child on the outskirts of Boston. Her seducer, a decent young man, took the baby from her in order to provide it a decent upbringing. But the baby, missing his mother, died.

Then Polly's father died, and she inherited $2,000 from his estate, and this brought her to the attention of Ned Findley, a young man of little education and fewer morals, "unenlightened and depraved." They married, and she happily slaved for him, but he held her in little esteem, blows taking the place of caresses. Eight weeks after their marriage, she set out with him in a canoe to visit, he said, neighbors. Hardly were they afloat than he beat her across the shoulders and over the head with his paddle, knocking her overboard to drown. Of course, he was hanged.

"Fond parents," Weems pleaded, "think of poor Findley and tremble for your sons." Do better in Christian nurture than his parents had done for him. "Preachers, look up to the gibbet and mourn," for you have not done your task well. "Generous Legislators! lament the curses of education" badly managed. "Young man . . . Fortune hunters . . . fair daughters of wealth . . . think of poor Polly and tremble."

Though more space is given to Findley and his upbringing that encouraged brutality, the spotlight focusses most clearly on Polly, and not so much on her unhappy lot as on the unnatural, unfeeling, and unChristian cruelty of parents who fail to realize that the greater a daughter's folly, the greater must be the parent's pity and sympathetic understanding: "Think of the joy when you shall see your once fallen daughter rais'd to a glorious saint."

Had Polly been properly schooled and furnished with books, she might have been saved. For "God is love," and the sustaining backbone of the family is love, not cruelty and anger. Forgiveness and forbearing must be the Christian parent's first duties. Jesus and Mary Magdalene must be remembered. The words of Christ must supplant the ways of men. Parson Weems flung his rhetoric wide as he pleaded for sympathy and understanding.

And Ned had no chance either. Born and brought up in a backcountry village, he had been conditioned to rapacity and cruelty. In describing old Edgefield as it had been in Ned Findley's boyhood, Weems anticipates so many themes and devices later to be developed in the literature of the South, indeed in the literature of nineteenth-century America, that the wonder is that literary historians have not made more of him.

In old Edgefield, people had "no more notion of *restraint* than the Indians, and if only touched by the trammels of law, would jump and kick like so many colts or a young Zebra hitched to a wagon." They were a lawless people: "a tough pull of the snout was *all one* as an indictment—a broken head passed current for a capital indictment—and a stunning knock to the ground *settled the hash*, like the foreclosure of a mortgage." If one listens carefully, Mark Twain's voice may be heard, certainly the more raucous voice of Augustus B. Long-street who thirty years later in *Georgia Scenes* recounted country high jinks.

One bumptuous Edgefieldian who thought himself to have been badly treated by a local magistrate came bouncing out of the courthouse "like a shot out of a shovel . . . ripping and tearing about the yard like a wild man!"—and not unlike Mark Twain's unfortunate Mr. Boggs—"damning both judges and jury for all the pick pocket sons of b-tches he could think of! daring them to come out, *only to come out,* and he would show them, God *damn 'em,* what it was to give a *judgment against a gentleman like him!*"

During court days "you might see the poor *blackguards* by the dozen, with battered jaws and bung'd eyes, poking like blind dunghill cocks on a Soft-Tuesday. . . . Here you might have heard the BULLIES hard at it; some laying on each other like horses; others like drunken Negroes, bawling out at every blow. *Hurra Ben!—Lay on! Lay on! give it to him Dick! . . . Mind your cross buttock! hurra! up he goes!—now's your time—Gouge! gouge! damn you, why don't you gouge!*"

Weems's change of tone was rapid, again mixing vulgarities of the tavern with the elevated pieties of the pulpit, blending voices or using them antiphonally, though not as successfully as Mark Twain would. Sometimes he can be thought to anticipate Joel Chandler Harris, who half a century later would allow Uncle Remus to tell animal fables, as, for example, his inserting into this tale of careless love and brutal murder an account of how the fox gets rid of fleas, to wit:

"When that wily little rogue finds that he has more live stock about him than he wishes to winter, he snaps a good mouthful of wool from the first briar patch he comes to, and going to a pond, very leisurely lets himself down into the water, still holding the wool in his mouth. The fleas, who are mortal haters of cold water, finding they are like to be swamped, immediately take the track to pull for life on the Fox's belly and sides. Reynard still goes down—and as he goes down, they go up. Still chased by the water they continue to travel upward till at length coming to the land's end of his snout, they trap off into the stick of wool. No sooner has Reynard found that his company were all safe aboard, then wishing them bon voyage, he dodges his nose under the water and so clears himself."

Fables were fine, but slander was not. Some of the people of Edgefield did not take kindly to the way that Weems had portrayed their roughhouse antics. Once, it has been said, while travelling cautiously through backcountry Georgia, where some of the "more angry boys" had "threatened revenge on the parson," his wagon bogged down in a quagmire "from which his unassisted strength utterly failed to extricate it. He was miles from habitation, the road was an obscure one, and the day was failing." So, taking his violin from its case, he "took his seat on a log by the side of the road and proceeded to exhort from the wood and catgut such strains as . . . would have mocked the best fantasies" of the fabled fiddler, Ole Bull.

"This drew to him an audience. Two wandering backwoodsmen suddenly emerged from the covert, thoroughly charmed on the spot by the old man's music. They asked him many questions," but he did not give his identity away, only answered their questions by a more strenuous and melodious stroking of his bow. "They were satisfied with his responses," the story concludes, "and he was thus able to escape safely from the dangerous precincts. 'I took precious care,' said he, 'to say nothing of my name. When they pressed the question, my fiddle drowned their words, and my own too.' "

He may partially have assuaged the wrath of these backcountry Georgians by publishing another pamphlet, *The Devil Done Over; or the Grand Revival in Old Edgefield in 1809*, in which he explained how in that district "seven hun-

dred souls were added to the Baptist Church in nine Months,"
but that pamphlet seems to have sold less widely than his
earlier account of horrendous adventures.

The second of Weems's Hogarthian tracts, *God's Revenge
against Gambling*, written in Augusta, Georgia, in the late fall
of 1811, was lugubriously dedicated to Weems's oldest son,
Jesse, who was so many miles away and "so many are the
dangers and deaths that lurk between him and me" that perhaps "he will see my face no more; nor ever again hear my
voice talking to him about the happiness of BEING GOOD. Well,
then, I will send him this little book. Perhaps its rustling
leaves may one day speak to him of me . . . from its tear-
dropped pages he may hear his father's voice thus crying in
his ear," that the gambler's way "IS THE WAY OF HELL, GOING
DOWN BY THE CHAMBERS OF DEATH."

But there are few rustling leaves in this little book. It opens
with a whirlwind jeremiad of a kind more characteristic of a
seventeenth-century New England divine than of the love-
dispensing Parson Weems. God has stalked with great anger
through our Southern states, he said. "Lashed by furious
winds, the sea has risen up from her dark and horrid bed, and
bursting over her sandy barriers with a mountain swell . . .
has spread dismay and desolation along all our coasts, Sharks
and sea-monsters have sported over the cotton fields of our
pride . . . the *tornado*, too, with a fury never equaled in the
memory of man, has raged through our land with a mile wide
sweep, leveling every thing before it . . . bursting thunder
through the forests, leaving hideous lanes behind it, of pros-
trate oaks, and pines torn up by the roots, or snapped off
at the trunk like stick-weeds. . . . The caterpillar . . . has
been set forth from his secret places" to attack "our cotton
fields and gardens. . . . But, more dreadful still, the *pestilence* under the name of yellow fever, has been let loose on
our fairest cities."

This was all true enough, for the South Atlantic States had

been buffeted by early autumn storms, and yellow fever had run rampant among the people there. Were these judgments of God? Yes, said Weems, but God's judgments, rightly understood, can be blessings. They cannot be understood by people like Calvinists, of New England or anywhere else, who believe "that there are millions of sweet little babies, *not a span long*, broiling in hell flames, and there to continue to broil and scream to all eternity for *God's glory!* can hardly see God's judgments in the right light. Such horrible notions of God cannot otherwise than throw a correspondingly horrible colouring over all his dispensations," which, seen rightly, are blessings.

Weems then takes a mighty pulpit plunge into what may seem a nonsequitur, explaining that God's love and concern for his people must be translated as love among his people. His ways are indeed wondrous, and difficult to explain. But this can be known, that God created the human family to be as one great social body, of which every person is a member, and to which every person is bound to contribute his part "as *service*," and "in turn receive from it his share of safety and comfort."

But, "alas! the gambler is blind to all such beautiful ideas." A "sordid groveling wretch! Himself, himself is all he cares for; provided he wins, no matter who sinks.—Hence his life is a shameful discordance from the universal harmony." And the gambler always loses. They take from, but do not contribute to God's earthly family, bound by love. And to what avail? Who ever heard of a gambler dying rich?

Take the case of poor Gilmore, once so fine a young man, but whose "excesses created debts, debts begat duns, and duns begat sorrows. To rid himself of his wretchedness he went at once to the gambling table, which quickly swallowed up his estate, and reduced his wife and little son to poverty." Finally repentant, while his wretched wife "was toasting a crust of bread for his breakfast . . . he took down his gun, placed it against his forehead, and touching the trigger with his toes, scattered his brains over the ceiling, and fell by the side of his child half drowned in his father's blood."

Or consider young Tom Tittle, of Culpeper, Virginia, the spoiled and only son of doting parents, who went one day to Fredericksburg where, "having no book in his pocket to amuse him" while his mother and sister went shopping, "strolled into a gambling room" where, after losing all of his property and having mortgaged some of his father's also, he was led by his nose to the door "and kicked . . . into the street." Remorseful, "he took the halter from one of his horses, and went and hung himself." Or remember young Thomas Alston, of Halifax, North Carolina, who thinking himself cheated by gamblers, waylaid one of them by the side of the road, who "blowed out the brains of the unfortunate Alston."

But "why should we mourn for *one*," asked Weems, "when thousands and millions" are "the bleeding victims of their sin," the prey of the professional sharpster who is none more than "a miserable OUT-LAW sneaking from town to town, from the *cock-fight* to the *horse-race* with cards and dice in his pocket, seeking of what fools with lean brains and fat purses he can besmear," fleecing men like Drisden Harwood of Maryland or reckless maidens like pretty Frances Braddock—for women were not exempt from folly—who sacrificed "her bloom, her beauty, her fame and fortune . . . to the most *detestable of vices*," and finally, wrapping her silken girdle around her neck, "hung herself over the door of her chamber."

The dreadful vice of gambling attracted, not only the careless and the beautiful, but also no less a person than Maria Antoinette of France, who "was but a humming bird, decked with the liveliest colours . . . flapping from flower to flower of gaiety and dissipation." Her gambling table was notorious. What fortunes were squandered there! How many courtiers were there ruined, their wives and children beggared! But

God's justice prevailed: "hurled from throne to prison, and thence dragged to the guillotine, her unpitied head was struck off. . . . And her dead body thrown, naked into the ditch and covered with quick-lime, was presently dissolved into a loathsome jelly."

Better poor than enriched by gambling. Consider the apple woman contentedly selling her wares by the roadside, her ruddy-faced children beside her. Or the farmer who, with his sons, patiently tills his few acres. "The pupils of Hoyle," said Weems, "may smile" at such "simple annals of the poor," but, if gaming prevailed, "the whole country would be filled with poor uneducated children, naked and crying for bread."

What a great satisfaction it is, to be "living in a country like this, where millions of acres untouched by the plough" are "cheap as dirt—a country in which every lovely woman would make an excellent wife" with whom a man "could sit down so happily," while "all bounteous nature smiled around him," his "fields adorned with corn and cotton," and his "meadows affording pasture for sweet-breathed cows—the hills sustaining his fleecy flocks; the orchards for savory fruits—the woods for winter's firing and summer's shade." Here, his "tender wife and sweet prattling children" beside him, was paradise indeed, an agrarian paradise where God rewards honest labor.

But Satan has also been here at work. Pickpockets, horse-thieves, and gamblers roam this goodly land. They loot, and they tempt. At first, a person may play at cards only for pleasure: "It was only a *civil game*, and where was the harm in that?" Winnings might be contributed to church or charity. But for every winner, there is a loser, desperate perhaps to get back the money that should have gone for his children's food. The "horrible bewitchments" of gambling means empty coffers at home, hungry children, and bewildered wives. "Thus every year are cut off in their bloom thousands of poor deluded youth, who, but for the sin of gambling, might have sustained the glorious character of *'Fellow labourers with God,'* in his blessed work of making the world happy."

There are no rich gamblers, not in any sense.

The Drunkard's Looking Glass that appeared a year later was a less gloomy book. A reader will suspect that Weems himself enjoyed an occasional social nip. "Drink no longer water," he advises, "but use a *little* wine for the stomach's sake. Also cider, ale, beer," and he advises, as if from experience, "Hot coffee in the morning is a good cure for *dram-craving*. And a civic crown to him who will set the fashion of *coffee* at dinner."

This looking glass is meant to reflect, he tells us, "a faithful likeness of the drunkard in sundry very interesting attitudes, with lively representations of the many strange capers which he cuts at different stages of his disease." On the title page, he identifies the several stages of drunkenness, the *"first,* when he has only 'a drop in his eye,' *second,* when he is 'half-shaved,' *third,* when he is getting 'a little on the staggers or so,' and *fourth* and *fifth,* and so on, till he is 'quite capsized' or 'snug under the table with the dogs,' and 'can't stick to the floor without holding on.'"

But in the text, he speaks only of three stages: the "Frisky or Foolish Stage," in which a person is likely to do more harm to himself than to others, the "Frantic or Demonic Stage," which can render a person sometimes a deadly menace to other people, and the "Stupid or Torpid Stage," when he finally topples to the floor like a wet dish mop. Like Benjamin Franklin before him, he identifies terms used to identify a tippler: boozy, groggy, blue, damp, tipsy, fuddled, haily gaily, how come you so, half shaved, swipy, has got a drop in his eye, cut, has got his wet sheet abroad, cut in the crew, and, in Georgia, high up to picking cotton.

"But tho' so different in name, 'tis the same nature, all but one disease still." And its results are plain, for all to see.

Whether an imbiber has been "at a Funeral or a Wedding, a Horse-race or cock-fight, a Corn-husking, or a Quilting match . . . the symptoms of his disease are visibly all over him. Every feature is a tell-tale; every grin and stare betrays him. Only look at his eyes, see how they twinkle!—his *cheeks*, how they swell and redden!—and, Oh! that eternal chatter-box his *tongue!*—His head, his legs, his feet are all in tantrums; he can't sit still, but must be upon the floor cutting his capers; he throws out his arm; snaps his fingers; and striking in to a shuffle, round and round the room, he goes singing and sailing and singing with his head upon his shoulder, nodding and leering all the while, with a most disgusting simper on his face. Presently up he runs, seizes you by the head, jerks you out upon the floor, and striking up some jig tune, sets into dancing as hard as he can, and staring you in the eyes most odiously sweet.

"You are now in a bad box; for if you take no notice of him at all, he is sure to turn mad, and give you a confounded knock on the head. And if on the other hand, you return his loathsome compliments, he becomes ten fold loathsomer still. He seizes you around the waist, and like a drunken ape, gives you such a hug as though he would hug the breath out of your body; and while he is poisoning you to death with his stinking breath, he continues to bawl out that you are '*a d----d clever fellow,*' and swears by his Maker that '*he loves you like h-ll.*' "

Then Weems tells the tale of a "posse of younkers" in Alexandria, who "having despatched their oysters, and dismissed the shells . . . gathered around the table and bravely set in to *drink*, filling up the short intervals with fragrant segars and jovial songs. By midnight their youthful blood was much too hot for the dining room, and out they darted into the street for cool air and *mischief*." They removed the sign from the barber's shop, "SHAVE HERE FOR HALF A BIT," and hung it over the lawyer's door, and over the parson's door they hung a sign that promised "CAKES AND BEER FOR SALE HERE."

Then "after cutting a number of such wild capers, they came at length on a squadron of Carts that were lying near one of the wharves by the river—'dam' me boys!' cried their file-leader, 'here's fun for us! Let's chuck these Carts into the River, there'll be OLD CURSING here in the morning among the Car-men.'" And there was cursing indeed when the magistrate made each of the young men pay "a pretty round sum, for smart money.

"One of my young relatives who took part in the scrape," said Weems, "told me that *his part* came to ONE HUNDRED DOLLARS."

He then told of the serio-comic high jinks of a young clergyman who, warmed by wine, dared the company to do everything that he did. Would they have the courage to follow the leader? They did, and as he threw his clothes, one by one into the fire, they followed "until the blushing fools all huddled together around it naked as they were born!" And he told of a lawyer "who in a drunken frolic was miserably unsuited," and of a physician who in his cups talked himself into an ill-fated duel, of a handsome headstrong young Irishman who did the same, and of a young bricklayer who "skipped into a carpenter's shop" and reached his hand for what he thought to be a whiskey bottle but which turned out to be a caustic, so that he went off "as with a dram of hell-fire in his throat," and of a young sailor staggering down the street, "as happy as an Admiral" until "unluckily capsized, fell head long into a cellar," never to rise again:

> Old Parson, he preached for tythes O!
> Our Lawyer he prattles for prog;
> Our Doctor, he blisters—as you know,
> But hang 'em, they all love the grog.

Many of the results of such tippling are presented with a comic touch. Indeed Weems asked Mathew Carey to find for him, if he could, a frontispiece "of the funny sort," though he also asked him to look for drawings of "drunken characters . . . haggard and distemperd. . . . Let their Carbuncles show disease & disgrace." For if he were to attract readers by his wit, that wit might also lead toward wisdom as they considered the dreadful results of gin-inspired pleasures.

Sometimes he presented them with a set piece, like his description of the people gathered to enjoy the sport, and more besides, at Noyle Nelms's race-paths. Notice of the event had been "given by plentiful advertisements stuck up, as usual, at blacksmith's shops, taverns, and cross roads. At length the *eventful day* arrived; and the neighbourhood, for miles around, quitting their spinning-wheels and ploughs, are all in motion to see the *races!* By an early hour the piney wood, which surrounds the race-paths, is filled with a motley croud—*yonder*, the delicate daughters of wealth, lolling at ease in their silks and chariots, waiting for the starting of the horses; and here the sturdier daughters of poverty, standing together in giggling groups, shining in health and homespun.

"On *this side*, a gang of smirky-faced negroes, each with his whiskey bottle sticking out of his pocket—and on *that* a troop of broad grinning Indians, with their brandy kegs and children strapped over their shoulders—while in rows, along the course, stand the whiskey wagons and cyder carts, surrounded by thirsty topers, thick as bees, all *sipping away as hard* as the smiling tapsters can fill, and hand them their tin pots and noggins. Presently the fiery draughts begin to operate; dull care unbends from every brow; and all the tongues are loosened to chatter; for honest Nature, now unmuzzled by the whiskey, throws off restraint, and bids every man appear in his proper character.

"Some are singing—and some are dancing; *here*, they hug and fondle like brothers—*there* they curse and quarrel like enemies. The negroes laugh—the Indians whoop—and all the woods resound with uproar. No flock of black-birds lighting on an autumnal cornfield, ever raised such a chorus of ear distracting sounds."

But then a fight breaks out as "a couple of big-limbed boobies" rush into furious battle, pitching at each other "like bulldogs. The contest, however is of short duration; for, one of the fools, in taking his dose of Dutch courage, had gone so deep into the whiskey bottle, that he was quite on the staggers, when the fight began; so that on the first or second thump he was tumbled over sprawling and helpless as a cotton bag. Whereas his antagonist . . . leaped into the air, and snapping his fingers roared out, '*Hurra, for me! a hard horse I am gentlemen, a proper hard horse, depend! may-be I an't a* ROARER!'"

And then another fight began. One boisterous roisterer "*d--ns himself* to h-ll, IF HE CAN'T FLOG ANY SON OF A B-TCH ON THE WHOLE GROUND." Another roars, "Here I come gentlemen! . . . *Here I come! a screamer! yes d--n me, if I an't a proper screamer; just from* BENGAL! HALF HORSE HALF ALLIGATOR, AND WITH A LITTLE TOUCH OF THE SNAPPING TURTLE." Then still another boasts, "I'll *be d--n'd if I an't a* TRUE STUD. O, *may be I an't a Roarer.*"

Then into the midst of this raucous crew, up dashes "poor Dred Drake, with red eyes and whiskey-bloated face," astride "a high mettled Tacky, and screaming out, '*Clear the track! clear the track! d--n you, clear the track.*'" And off he dashes, "a piney-wood sot—no hat—no jacket—and his uncombed locks flying in every direction in the wind." Poor Dred Drake, on he rode. "His horse under the lash, as hard as he could crack it, rather flying than running, started a little from the path, and in full lightning speed, dash'd his rider against the body of a pine tree. Knocked backwards, high above his horse's rump," poor Dred fell dead. "There was no sign of a nose remaining on his face, the violence of the blow had crushed it flat." One of his eyes "was clearly knocked out of its socket; and, held only by a string of skin, there it lay naked on his bloody cheek."

Such were the fatal effects of drinking. And Weems had other examples in plenty to illustrate its awful effects. The sad story of the misadventures of John and Peter Hay in "yielding themselves up the slaves of drunkenness, and for so ignoble a vice tarnishing their long respected names," was so well received that he printed it, and in more than one edition, in a little pamphlet of its own that sold wondrously well.

> Thus lips that do with brandy burn,
> Shall never prosper long;
> God's righteous vengeance shall consume
> The whiskey loving tongue.

How wasteful was this awful vice! Weems knew of one man who spent six dollars a day, "in one week upwards of forty dollars," for food and drink and pleasure, his daily expenses being:

To 3 mint slings before breakfast, 25	75
1 breakfast	50
9 tumblers of grog before dinner	1 12½
3 glasses of wine and bitters 12½	37½
Dinner and Club	1 25
2 Tickler and French brandys 25	50
Segars	25
Supper and wine	1 25
	$6 00

And "for all this waste of substance," he "carries home to his wife and children nothing but a *red nose!*"

But there is one "True Cure for Drunkenness." Having submitted himself to its alleviating power, no man need ever again be impelled to step to the sideboard, where seizing "the dear decanter by the neck, and pouring out a *four fingered*

bumper," he "tosses it off with scarcely here's to ye, and re-
peats the stupifying dose until he loses his legs, and sinks
beneath the brutal point." Solomon had wisely observed that
people drink *"to forget their sorrows* and remember their
misery no more." Therefore, "Parents! Legislators! and
Preachers! would you make the nation sober, make them
happy: to make them *happy* study their nature."

For "man's nature is *threefold*. He is at the same time animal, intellectual, and divine." To make him happy, "which is
the only way to make him sober," he must be taught to know
the pleasures of sense, of knowledge, and divine love. Exercise and industry, education (and this need not be of the university kind), and recognition of the love and amiable goodness of God can provide assurance "that our sons shall never
be drunkards," for by these means "we keep them happy."

For "idleness is sorrow, and breeds Drunkards as naturally
as water breeds bull-frogs," and "ignorance is sorrow, and
has emptied many a rum hogshead." When John Wesley
preached among besotted and impoverished English miners,
"Rags gave way to goodly garments. Bread was seen and to
spare among the cheerful children."

Not "millions of *wrangling sermons* on Infant Baptism, or
Adult Baptism, on Freewill or Election have produced the
good" that Wesley did, in requiring for salvation only "Re-
pentance and *Faith working* by Love!" The Anglican Parson
Weems had travelled a long theological road, discovering that
its only signpost was love. "O who then among you will rise
up for God against this accursed sin of drunkenness that pro-
duces broken-hearted mothers, with their pale, hollow-eyed
children, naked and crying for bread." Let us substitute for it
"respectful temperance," built firm on happiness in God, in
whose train would follow "all the virtues tending to individual honour and domestic peace."

Beside the fervor and pictorial pungency of this tract
against drunkenness, *God's Revenge against Adultery* that

132

appeared in 1815 may seem tame indeed. It tells the sad stories of the accomplished Dr. Theodore Wilson, of Lewistown, "who for seducing Mrs. Nancy Wiley had his brains blown out by her husband," and of the elegant James O'Neale, Esq., of Wilmington, North Carolina, "who for seducing the beautiful Miss Matilda L'Estrange," was killed by her brother. Each was a seamy tale, meant to breed disgust. And each played on themes on which Weems had often played before.

Nancy Wiley, the wife of a good-natured Irish tavern keeper, was blessed—perhaps cursed—with beauty, her face as perfect as her form, but she lacked "the polish of a good education." She had been brought up "to accord with that silly old ballad which used to divert us in the *nursery*—

> And what's young women made of, made of?
> Pinks and roses, and such sweet posies, that's
>   what young women's made of.

James Wiley admired Dr. Wilson. The physician had once saved his life. And he suspected nothing of the doctor's friendship with his wife, "their *long evening walks together! their frequent ridings out in his gig!*" To friends who warned him of what was going on, he answered, "*Pshaw! the doctor is a finished gentlemen, sir, and I look on his attentions to my wife as a compliment to me.*" He might have guessed their guilty secret by his wife's altered attitude toward him, "for, as *no man can serve two masters,* no woman can love two men." Even "in the bed sanctified by Hymen, she would turn from him as in disgust and sigh like one whose heart was set upon some absent love."

And this provided Weems with an opportunity to insert a moralizing small anecdote, as pulpit practice had perhaps taught him, to delay the action and sharpen its claim that a truly good wife, true to the husband, "remains naturally indifferent" to all others. "*'Has not your husband a bad breath?'* said a demirep to a wife of this excellent sort. 'Indeed,' replied the lady very innocently, *'I don't know. I have never smelled any gentleman's breath but my dear husband's.'*"

But Nancy Wiley was not of this kind. One day her husband, "stepping accidentally into his chamber when it was thought by his wife that he had gone abroad . . . caught the doctor on a sofa with Mrs. Wiley on his lap. Leaning her cheek against his bosom, he encircling her in his arms and printing burning kisses on her lips." Again the story is interrupted, this time by an anecdote of a young man led astray by the allurements of Thomas Paine's aetheistic *The Age of Reason*, before the focus again returns to Wiley, who put a bullet through the doctor's head.

He was tried for murder. Saddened and maddened by his errant wife, he sought to kill her too, but was not allowed "to indulge in so diabolical a pleasure" by a relative who whisked her away. The doctor's lawyer brother attempted to shoot Wiley, but his pistol misfired. Wiley died in prison, and his wife, bereft of love, died also. The doctor's lawyer brother became a Presbyterian clergyman in Philadelphia: "Sin was the burden of his sermons."

The story of the seduction of Matilda L'Estrange by John O'Neale is more unified, a sentimental tale, to be sure, but with the kind of appeal that might make it, with few revisions, suitable for presentation among the true romances of almost any period. Matilda was the daughter of a wealthy farmer whose "riches were not of the hereditary and effeminate sort," but "were the brave and healthy offspring of his own virtues." Through his own labors, he had "swallowed up the land and negroes and flocks and herds of many of his lazy, dram drinking, gambling neighbors."

But wealth did not bring happiness. Something was lacking. So in his fifties, "he took up his Bible, and read it over with great care. He there discovered the reason why he had never been happy . . . that true happiness is to be found in God alone."

So "he invited neighbouring preachers, who were principally *methodists*, to come and preach at his house," inviting all people of the countryside to join with him and his family in devotions. All came, "not only the *poor* and the *mean*, but the *rich* and the *fair*." His daughter Matilda was especially drawn to the glories of salvation there held forth. An exuberant girl, she shared her joy at having been led toward divine truths by throwing her arms around family and friends, exclaiming, "I am converted! . . . I am happy. I am so happy."

Among fellow communicants was James O'Neale, a married man. "But, alas, Mr. O'Neale was not that *spiritual* brother which this fair saint supposed; and her virgin carresses instead of exciting the pure transports of angelic sympathy, only served to kindle . . . the fever of brutal passion." Taking advantage of her innocent transports, he seduced her.

She was not turned out by her heartbroken father, only sent by him to live with a neighboring aunt until after his death. Fearing that O'Neale might continue his attentions to the girl, her brother was sent each evening to sit with his sister and her aunt until bedtime. One night, starting home on foot through the forest that separated his father's lands from those of his aunt, he came on O'Neale and filled his body with buckshot.

The villain died "in horrors unutterable." The brother was tried and convicted, but was pardoned by the Governor of the State of North Carolina. But Matilda's brokenhearted father died, and his widow was soon laid by his side in the grave; the brother died, as did Matilda's only sister. What happened to Matilda is not told.

Each of these small and enlightening and very popular

books was made on a single pattern. The tales which they contain, complete in themselves, are introduced and followed by admonition and instruction on the necessity for education, the duty of parents to provide proper religious instruction and also proper examples to their children, and on the advantages of reading as a protection from evil. They are, again, edifying tales, such as a preacher might tuck into a sermon, but they are more unified than in the less well focused narratives embedded in the story of Delia or in *Hymen's Recruiting Serjeant*. They also, and always, contain a bookseller's sales pitch: Read more books.

In the *Virginia Patriot* of Richmond in February, 1818, Weems presented for the first time a story which is apparently complete in itself, pointing toward a moral, but with no moral explicitly attached. It was called "Good News from the Devil, or the Precious Fruits of a Popshop," and it played on fears of slave insurrections that worried people after the War of 1812, and played also on the duty of masters properly to educate their slaves, not necessarily in learning, but in proper ways of Christian behavior.

The story is horrendous. The narrator, riding in a coach toward some Southern town, sees "a HUMAN BEING (a negro of gigantic size) hanging up in chains by the roadside! The birds had plucked his eyes from their darkened sockets; his flesh, like blackest parchment, clave to his bones while his teeth, chalky white and clenched in the large extended jaws, resembled Death himself, gnashing with rage that he had not his dart and liberty to murder the frightened passengers."

A travelling companion explained who the poor fellow was and why he was there. His name was Dick, and his owner had allowed "him to run very much his own master." Dick was attracted to a popshop, a dram shop, run by an unscrupulous white man. There he learned to drink and was taught to gamble, losing his self-respect and all the small possessions that he had.

136

In drunken stupor, he planned revenge. He would kill the popshop owner, his wife, his children, and the wife's mother. All escaped except the latter and two drunken louts who snored on the pophouse floor. These three were brutally bludgeoned to death with a heavy pothook that Dick snatched from the pophouse fireplace.

Dick was, of course, caught and hanged. His story is told with considerable realistic but gory gusto, and stands as a thing in itself—except that appended to it is a notice that anyone who wishes to know more about the evils and dangers of drunkenness will do well to purchase *The Drunkard's Looking Glass*, the 5th edition, with two cuts, which was for sale along with other writings by M. L. Weems in the lobby of the House of Delegates. In one way or another, Weems would see to it that his books sold.

Two years later, Washington Irving in "The Legend of Sleepy Hollow" and "Rip Van Winkle" would present stories as stories, without protruding moral instruction, and James Fenimore Cooper would soon attract readers with tales of forest life and Indian ways without the author pointing toward what should be thought about what happened. But Weems remained a devoted parson to the end, a person who spoke bluntly and to the point about backslidings toward evil ways.

He was a person with a mission. If that mission was to sell books, it was also to warn of snares that could entrap the unwary. He knew his audience, and he played to its requirements well.

God's Revenge against Duelling, or the Duellist's Looking Glass in 1820 was advertised as "admirably calculated to entertain and instruct the American youth." It contained no less than thirty examples of how that silly practice denied all control over *"good sense, true courage,* and *real honor,"* as its author attempted "to open the eyes of a Devil-blinded world that they may see that the spirit of duelling, in place of

137

being a Sweet Gale from Heavenly Honor as is villainously intended, is a blast of Hellish Hate and Revenge." His touch was meant to be light, "For ridicule shall frequently prevail to cut the knot where graver reasons fail." But the light touch did not fit well with the seriousness of Weems's intentions. The examples of ruined lives, weeping wives, and orphaned children become tediously repetitious, so that the pamphlet seems to have been the least successful, certainly the least memorable of Weems's tracts.

But not *The Bad Wife's Looking Glass, or God's Revenge against Cruelty to Husbands* that appeared two years later, and just three years before its author's death. Sandwiched between many pages of moralizing and patiently repeated instruction on how children should be nurtured is the remarkable story of "the beautiful but depraved" Mrs. Rebecca or Becky Cotton.

Becky was "one of the prettiest nymphs that ever stole away from the preacher the eyes of Swains, causing those to sigh who came to pray." But, however pretty, she was not "blest with an enlightened mind," and her eyes, "though bright, lacked that all animating intelligence which kindles the beholder into admiration." Her parents, in short, had not given her a proper Christian upbringing. While still in her teens, she married a shiftless ne'er-do-well named John or Johnny Cotton, who spent more time in chewing tobacco, swilling grog, and loitering in taverns than in Christian husbandly duties. When ruffians came to confront Becky's father with having defrauded them and, then, in drunken anger, murdered him, her husband raised no hand to prevent them. This angered Becky, and she sought revenge.

Not even Lizzie Borden would manage better than Becky did. One evening, she approached her besotted husband, axe in hand: "She drove at his defenseless head a furious blow, which lighting immediately on his temple, bursted the skull and sunk deep into his brain." Then, aided by her little brother

Davy, "she dragged the corpse of her husband to a small meat house . . . and leaving him retired to bed. After *indulging in a nap!* she arose and returned to the meat house to see whether he was quite dead or not. Thinking that she saw him move an eye, she tied a rope around his neck, and throwing the other end over a rafter, drew him up from the ground, and there leaving him half hanging, went to her bed again." A little before daybreak, she woke and, again assisted by Davy, "dragged the corpse into the garden and buried it in an empty potatoe vault, covering the grave carefully with straw."

To inquisitive neighbors, she explained that Johnny was away on a business trip. But, "knowing what a *cat* and *dog* life" she and her husband had lived, the neighbors became suspicious. A reluctant but repentant young Davy led them to the corpse in the potato vault.

Becky was tried for murder, but her beauty so impressed the jury that she was acquitted, and one of the jurors, a wealthy retired major, took her into his household and, not long later, married her. She took over the Major's financial affairs and managed them to her own benefit, and she spoiled the attempts of another of her brothers, named Stephen, to marry one of the Major's pretty daughters, and she robbed Stephen of money that he had invested in one of the Major's enterprises. So Stephen picked up a large stone and clunked her over the head. She died unrepentant, but provided an object lesson to all who thought that beauty alone could triumph over morality.

Had Becky been brought up according to Christian principles, none of this need have happened. Many pages are directed, before and after the story of her horrid adventures, to parents who fail to provide a proper education to their children. Weems had apparently been criticized for his sometimes quite too vivid descriptions of wrongdoing. "But how," he now asks, "can the world learn wisdom unless those cruel *deeds* be *published* which provide God's judgments. And to what end so worthy were writing and printing taught to mankind?" He was grateful that he was "frequently, even daily receiving thanks from the Bishops & Clergy, as well as from Patriots & Philanthropists of all Professions & Ranks, for our Moral Looking Glasses." He hoped that they, together with his "moralizing biographies" would "help many a poor child to early wisdom, and Patriotism & Honor!"

Then, "let us take heed, good Reader, how we get angry with a writer when we have reason to believe that his main object, from God's judgments on Man's curses, [is] to enforce that *substantial morality* which is the grand pattern of individual and national security." The humble story of Becky and her difficulties was, he explained, only "a drop into the . . . Ocean of moral instruction." As far as can be determined, these are the last words written by Parson Weems to explain what his writings were about. Jonathan Edwards or many other Puritan divine might in an uncautious moment have said the same.

9. *"I Have Ever Glowed with a Book Vending Enthusiasm"*

uring all the years that Mason Locke Weems was writing biographies and moral tracts, he was still, year in and year out, on the road, selling books. That he thought to be his principal vocation. Writing was chiefly done to provide the kinds of books that experience taught him that people needed, and would buy. He pretended little pride in authorship, but, my, how he did like to hear his writings praised as useful!

"I have ever glowed with a book vending enthusiasm," he had confided to Mathew Carey. "I believe in the immortality of the Soul, and the future reign of Light, Liberty & Love. I believe too that . . . those who have aided the diffusion of Light and Love shall outshine the stars. Hence my enthusiasm to vend good books."

Back again in harness with Mathew Carey, after 1807, he was off to a new start. In spite of being hindered "by so many obstacles, bad roads, bad weather, high freshes, & the Dear knows what," he thought then of extending his territory, even into Tennessee and Kentucky. He had visions still of a network of bookstores and libraries throughout the South, all stocked with useful volumes. Through them, a fortune might be made, perhaps as much as ten or fifteen dollars a day.

Again he and Carey bantered and bickered. Do send me the right books, said Weems, not the outscourings of your storeroom. Send me books that will sell, and at the right price: a ninepence in hand is better than a shilling let slip. Let me have useful books, on the care of horses, the cultivation of kitchen gardens, books on quilting and preserving, and simple medical books with recipes for antibilious pills, worm lozenges, ague drops, itch ointments, and "the far worse worms of envy & vice." Had he time, he would write them himself.

The embargo of 1809 and then the War of 1812 had made money short, so that sales had declined, and spirits as well. The war especially had bothered him: "The modern Goths, our Enemy think it no harm to employ, rockets, bombs, and red hot shot." So he had written to President Madison, offering a solution for an end to that war. "Why not follow their example?" he asked, and he offered a plan to do away at once with invading forces; "I w^d turn the whole force of all saving Gunpowder against them," he wrote, by filling tarred canvas hose with gunpowder and laying it "in deep furrows run by a narrow plough." He was certain that a "few thousand yards of this hose laid at convenient distances along which the spoilers of our towns must march" would "in a moment annihilate their Troops and their hopes. The thing," he assured Madison, "is most easily practicable."

The war had ended without the use of his ingenious device—though the same, conceived by later artful minds, was used with some success on enemy convoy routes and airfields during World War II. After the war, much of Weems's travelling for several years was confined to what he thought of as his northern territory, Maryland and Virginia, with only occasional sorties into the deeper South.

As he grew older, travelling became increasingly difficult, even with his son Jesse occasionally available to help him, the father dashing ahead in a light carriage to make sales—sometimes dashing quite too fast, thought Carey, so that his horse was too often lamed—and the son lumbering behind in a heavily loaded wagon to make deliveries. Mrs. Weems worried about her young son on the road, fearful that he might succumb to the lure of tobacco or strong drink.

Roads continued to be rough and springs were inadequate,

so that "tossing and tumbling" through the mountains of Virginia, "and in a miserable hard riding gig," brought on "a severe hemorroidal complaint" that had Weems for days "tossing & squalling chairbound at home." Winds and rains brought on chills and catarrhs that defied medication. You have no idea, he told Carey, of the hardships of a book vendor's life.

But he pressed on, "wet, cold, feverish, thirsty, hungry," through "bad roads, wintry weather, floods." Not "robbers, fatigue, unprofitable labours, wasting life," nor worries about his "indigent family" ever quite dampened his book vending enthusiasm, particularly in the sale of his own "Serio comical melodramatic" pamphlets that warned against the perils of gambling, drinking, duelling, and marital infidelities. Of books of this kind, "thousands of great men every where tell me," he said, "you can't multiply too many copies."

He was increasingly impressed by great men. Every President, from Washington through Monroe, with the curious exception of John Adams, received and commented on copies of these books, most of them saying something politely flattering that could be used in furthering sales.

Weems had a great and exciting time during the early winter of 1820 hobnobbing with President Monroe and his family—Mrs. Monroe was found to be especially gracious—and with members of the Congress, selling subscriptions to a grand, new Americanized edition of LeSage's historical atlas. He had never met, he said "with smiles more cordial." Rufus King was "wonderfully gracious" and promised to recommend Weems's biography of Washington "to the nation as the best book for children." But Weems found it hard to understand why John Quincy Adams, though he would subscribe for the atlas, asked to be excused from endorsing a book that he had not seen.

But heady as the experience was of rubbing elbows with the great in the nation's capital, South Carolina and Georgia continued to beckon as virgin territories in which books could be sold, and books written as well. From this time forward more time was spent in the deep South, sometimes with a wagon and a boy to drive it, with the salesman resting in comparative ease, sometimes in a light stage which could take them more swiftly into the back country. Having a driver relieved him, Weems said, "of much fatigue, so that I shall be able to continue my harrangues to the crowds at Court Houses to better effect—and be able to travel faster & in greater safety."

The arrival of his "Flying Library" to a country town was a public event, especially in Georgia where there was less competition for sales than in Charleston or Columbia, where bookshops were beginning to abound. He heralded its coming in the newspapers, offering "Books, Wisdom & Virtue to Georgia forever," and he gave public lectures reminding listeners that in "a happy republic like ours, where the prize of Fame and Fortune all start fair and fair alike, where every thing depends on merit, and that merit is all dependent on Education, it is hoped that wise & generous parents will need no persuasion to give their children those very great advantages that books afford." He promised a liberal allowance "to those benevolent characters who take several copies . . . for Christmas books to their young relations":

> God prosper long our noble state!
> In wisdom, Wealth, and Peace,
> And grant that reading, now too rare,
> May day by day increase.

Sometimes he had to travel alone. When he set out for home from Charleston in June, 1821, he reported that "friends here, who seem to be numerous, *all* shake their heads at mention of my traversing the low fenny country & rice swamps on my solitary way, saying I had better sell my horse & gig & come by water."

But few books could be sold on shipboard. So, though he was advised, he said "to make my will & order my coffin before I set out," he beat his way northward through rain and mud, at one time "completely engulphed in a Quagmire—both of the shafts of my gig broken, my horse and self within an ace of being drowned." He was weeks recovering in Dumfries from "the effects of the melting heat, fatigue & noxious miasmata" of that journey.

But by autumn, he was ready to be off again, his gig repaired, and stout new clothes acquired for the journey southward once more. He planned to spend the next two years in Georgia and South Carolina, finishing up the business of selling his stock of fine new Bibles and atlases. What if he did die there? "I may as well," he said, "go to the Society of Good People from that Country as Dumfries." He made his way slowly, stopping off at Raleigh, Hillsborough, and Chapel Hill in North Carolina, to sell books there. He hoped that on his return journey he could visit some of the resort places in the western part of that state where he could, he hoped, "refresh myself for a week or two & where I may get a great many subscriptions of the wealthy people that attend them."

But he did not return. "I shou'd like," he said, "to stay in these Southern States until I have done nearly all that cou'd be done" with the splendid Bible and the atlases. But what sold best were his own small books. "I am frequently, even daily receivg thanks from the Bishops & Clergy, as well as from Patriots & Philanthropists of all Professions & Ranks, for our Moral Looking Glasses." Afternoons were reserved for selling, for cajoling crowds, or visiting with people of distinction, but, he said, "I have no better way spending my evenings & mornings than in writing something for the good of youth."

When Mathew Carey suggested that time spent in composition was time stolen from selling, Weems exploded in exasperation that "if I had not a fondness to scribble to divert my thoughts from Distraction, what could possibly have kept me from hard drink, from Gambling," and cheating you of profit? Whatever was said of them, he was increasingly certain that his "moralizing Biographies . . . and the Moral Looking Glasses will help many a poor child to early wisdom, and Patriotism & Honor."

He was full of new ideas. He encouraged Carey to think of establishing a sporting magazine that would appeal "to all the Southern Nabobs," the "Grandees of Pleasure" on turf and track. In "A Card to the Gentlemen of the Jockey Club" in the *Charleston Times* in March, 1821, asking their patronage of the *American Pocket Farrier* which he had conveniently for sale, he presented a eulogy on "that noble animal," the horse, "in all his various uses to mankind: whether dragging the sacred plough, or rapidly flying with the mail stage—whether wantonly prancing before a stately coach bright with the sparkling beauties, or furiously dashing into the thickest battle," and who, "yet after all, suffering himself to be led by a child or beaten by a ragged slave." How to exalt his beauties and utilities—how to improve his form and constitution—all this was presented in a wholly American book, "not like the foreign farriers in pedantic language which few understand," but in native terms "equally simple and powerful."

In one way or another, he kept his name and his bargains in books before the public. As a reminder of the educational value of his atlas, he contributed to the newspapers of both Charleston and Atlanta in the spring of 1821 the "Memoirs of a Fine Girl," extolling the virtues of a school mistress in Ann Arundel County of Maryland who, "Sweetning the pap of science with the sugar and nutmeg of sister-like tenderness and patience . . . soon got her little pupils so fond of that heavenly food that their growth in learning became the theme of general conversation far and near," with the result that she had a new school built for her and became wealthy, "the mistress of an elegant fortune."

All of the "children of the different schools, as well as other persons, were respectfully invited" by a card in the *Savannah Georgian* to attend a splendid lecture on Education which the Rev. Mr. Weems "by request will deliver." And the *Charleston Courier* was happy to print a notice that in an endeavor "to enlighten the Public Mind & therefore exalt the Moral & Political Character, especially of the rising generation," Mr. Weems was happy to offer for sale a remarkably complete genealogical, historical, and geographical atlas.

That "truly valuable and benevolent man, and citizen," the Rev. Mr. Weems "pronounced an eloquent exhortation in a Masonic ceremony in Atlanta," where the Sabbath School Teachers of that city publicly thanked him for his contribution of $18.00 "to aid the operation of their school"; this is in the same issue of the *Georgian* that contained "A Card" calling attention to the Bibles that he had for sale. A letter "on the present happily increasing attention to education" in the *Charleston Courier* is followed by an endorsement by "the Bishop & other Literary Worthies of his 'American Atlas,' conveniently for sale at his "Flying Library." "Don't Let the Spark Go Out" commanded an essay in the *Courier* commending Weems's assiduous efforts to distribute Bibles and learning.

To the *Courier* in March, 1823, he contributed "A Tale of Times of Old," telling of "The Defeat of Major Weymiss, at Fish Dam Fork," expanding the story of that Scotsman who in his *Life of General Francis Marion* he had described as a Mohawk, destitute of any amiable traits. "I don't know how it will gee with the learned South Carolina historians," he wrote, "but I know it gees very well with the truth, as the facts were communicated to me a few weeks ago by one of the officers named."

As British forces under the command of the perfidious Weymiss came swarming "as thick as wild geese around stacks of rice," the American forces shot them down, and then "like their own generous rattlesnakes . . . retired with sullen joy into their darksome woods." Then Weems ends the story by telling of one "hearty old buck, who chewed tobacco and talked big," and who "in spite of all the brandy that was poured into him . . . kept his legs until sunset," when he fell "into such a powerful sleep that not all the din of battle . . . ever grazed him," and who, wakened at sunrise, seeing all the dead enemy around him, exclaimed, "Oh my blessed God! only to think of this! here have the bullets been flying thick as hail, cutting down them poor fellows like hopper-grass, and I lying here all the time drunk! dead drunk!"

No moral was appended. None was needed. But when the story was reprinted in the *Augusta Chronicle,* it was said that readers "will no doubt recognize their old friend, the Rev. M. L. Weems, whose 'antibilious pamphlets' have been extensively taken in our country, and we believe, in numerous instances with salutary effect."

It was from this later period that many of the tales told of the eccentricities of Parson Weems seem to have originated, passed on by the testimony of another romancer who remembered him, or remembered having remembered him from boyhood days in Charleston. William Gilmore Simms recalls that as Weems became better known in that region, he was sought after by "very worthy persons indeed," a group of whom one afternoon "awaited him in one of the good old stately abodes of the Ashley river," eager to meet the man of whom so many good things were said.

"Merry music refreshed them as they sat. The violin was speaking briskly, touched evidently by a master hand. . . . Little did they think who was the player. But the strains were approaching. Suddenly the door was thrown open, and in danced the fiddler. A white-haired venerable man, in night gown and slippers, with a cheerful, bright mercurial eye, and of a laughing, sunshiney countenance, the expression of which was merry like that of boyhood. This was Weems. The shock was terrible. The big wigs never recovered from the surprise. You might have brained them with a feather."

At another time, Simms recalled, when the "parson was one winter in Columbia," there "came a mountebank into the town, exhibiting feats of legerdemain. He had with him a musician, who constituted no inconsiderable part of his attraction. But the fiddler fell dangerously sick on the very day of the night set for the performance. He lodged at the same tavern with Weems. The good old parson heard of his predicament and went to him. He showed him his violin and gave him a few proofs of his mastery, and benevolently offered to play for him at the exhibition that night, only promising that a screen should be set to conceal his person. The stipulation was agreed to, and the night came. There was a large assemblage of people. The music proved to be of a superior order. The applause was tremendous, and the vanity of our biographer," Weems, "getting the best of him, he raised his head above the screen—thus making sure that the plaudits should not be wasted on the wrong person."

The prevalence of stories such as these put to question the assurances by Weems's descendants that he was no fiddler at all. Tradition proclaims him to have gathered bookbuying crowds as effectively with his jaunty music as with sermons or exhortations. He is said to have fiddled at weddings, when the fees for having solemnized the vows were still warm in his pocket. Whatever the fact, tradition remembers him as a merry fiddler. And he proved in his writings that truth might be disguised as fiction, and fiction take precedence over fact. He liked it there in the South, and more than once seems to have considered settling there permanently.

For all his efforts and energy and good will, as he moved into his sixties, his book vending enthusiasm finally waned. "My God," he wrote, "to think that with such a stock of knowledge aquir^d from 30 years of dear bought Experience—with such a heavy load of . . . zeal and enthusiasm to spread

149

that holy light of Morals & Politics, which best, and indeed alone can chase the Demons of Ignorance, Vice, Discord & Damnation from this young Republic."

With "such a Talent (so the good natur^d world says of me)," he continued, "for getting subscriptions to books—with such a flow of spirits to address Gaping Crowds (whether marshall^d on the Regimental muster Greens or pressing, thick as wild Turkies on the Court house pavements) on the advantages of Education—and the worth of Books—with such Health & unbroken nerves—such extensive acquaintances—and growing popularity, because of my moralizing productions—such rare opportunities & eagerness to establish Reading clubs & little Public libraries—such capacity for Auctioneering books; for receiving orders—for putting sub-[scription] papers in the safest & most influential hands—and such a fair chance for daily sales.

"I say that with all these advantages . . . such Patriotism—such Philanthropy—such Industry—such unequaled capacity for business—and yet! and yet! O Heavens! that these Mountains of Means shou'd not . . . have bro't even a mouse to market."

He was increasingly unwell, lonely and far from home, suffering with gout and rheumatism, and with an increasingly painful bladder complaint. He wondered whether it would be better to "wait a little to see what God will do," or whether Carey would not be wise to send another person to wind up their business in the South: "The doctor tells me that I am getting better, but I have my doubts."

He died at Beaufort, South Carolina, on May 23, 1825. His obituary described him as "a man of considerable attainments both as a scholar, a physician and divine." His eccentricities "were the eccentricities of genius and benevolence. He finally fell a martyr to his arduous exertions to do good."

He was buried at Beaufort, but his remains were later removed to a corner of the grounds at his home at Belle Air, just

DIED,

In Beaufort, S. C. on the 23d of May last, after a long and painful indisposition, the Rev. Mason L. Weems, of Dumfries, Va. well known as the author of the Life of Washington, and various other popular works, which have passed through numerous editions, and have had a most extensive circulation. He was a man of very considerable attainments both as a scholar, a physician and divine. His philanthrophy and benevolence were unbounded. Early in life he liberated his patrimonial slaves, from conscientious motives, and voluntarily commenced a career of incessant bodily toil, to disseminate moral and religious books in various remote and destitute portions of the country. From Pensylvania to the frontiers of Georgia was the principal theatre of his indefatigable labors, and it is supposed on good authority, that in the course of his life he has been instrumental in circulating nearly a million of copies of the scriptures and other valuable works. That in this laborious calling he was principally actuated by an expanded philanthropy, is proved by his entire neglect of the means of accumulating a large fortune and dying in comparative poverty. His very eccentricities, for failings they could not be called, were the eccentricities of genius and benevolence. He finally fell a martyr to his arduous exertions to do good, and died in the full enjoyment of faith, and a blessed hope of immortality.

Obituary of Weems
appearing in Raleigh, North Carolina, *Register*, July 23, 1825.

outside of Dumfries in Virginia. He did not outshine the stars, but he glowed, even twinkled, with amazing and amusing consistency. Known as one of nature's oddities, he was a goodly man withal.

His place is not among the literary great ones of his or any other generation. But he had his finger on the cultural pulse of a struggling young republic. In travelling up and down its coastal states, he probably came to know more people in more places than any other person of his generation. He wished them prosperity, and he sought to prosper himself by pointing toward means for success and reasons for failure. If in doing this he fed them much pap, it was in nourishing doses, palatable and exactly suited to what he considered to be their proper taste.

As a champion of what he thought to be right, he touched hearts, and he reminded heads that good conduct nurtured neighborliness and kept larders filled. He shared with many of his time the conviction that doing good could mean doing well, that honesty, industry, and moderation led toward prosperity, and that even geese, if properly taught, might indeed lay golden eggs.

APPENDIX:

WEEMS, THE BIOGRAPHER AND HISTORIAN
By William Gilmore Simms
from *Views and Reviews*, Second Series, 1845.

> A better Priest, I trowe, ther nowher non is,
> He waited after no pomp, no reverence,
> He maked him no spiced conscience,
> But Christes lore and his apostles twelve,
> He taught, but first he follwed it himselve.
> *Chaucer*

Some of your big-wigged gentry—your grave men . . . persons whom Nester himself could, under no circumstances, persuade to laugh,—will take it in high dudgeon that we should dignify under the title of historian, the lively "rector of Mount Vernon Parish."

History with this sort of persons, is a matter of very solemn concern. You are to approach it with bowed forehead, unbonnetted front, and most philosophical exordium. It is not your light romance—your irreverent poetry. It is a sort of holy revelation of the past. Hence, ye profane. Ye troubadours, be still, with your idle tenderness!—ye jongleurs, avaunt, with your mirthful minstrelsy!

There must be an awful solemnity of look and accent when the dry bones of ancient facts are to be unburied. You must delve, you must drudge, you must shake a mystical head, till it rattles again, in order to be a historian after the modern acceptation. You must discuss your problems, however insignificant, with a corresponding minuteness. You must show a becoming sense of what is due to their probable importance in the affairs of nations—which took no pains to preserve them. Shall Tweedledum succeed in the contest against Tweedledee, and shall there be no corresponding emphasis of utterance—no awful consciousness, on the part of the hurrying multitude, at the decision, for the future, of this long-vexed question.

The philosopher of history shudders at the humiliating conjecture. To him, the discovery of a fractional fact in the affairs of buried ages, though it concerns nothing of more weight than a cracked household vessel in the Palace of Calypso, is matter of graver import than the adjustment of a principle which involves the fate of a living people. The elucidation of an ancient cypher, or a fragment scrawl of papyrus, though it leads you no step farther, is matter of which to mould many volumes.

To such as these, solicitous in mere minutiae, toiling after the fact, though the fact be no ways important to the wholeness and the perpetuity of truth,—chronicling all things with Boeotian stolidity, and, by sheer force of gravitation, making painful an otherwise pleasant study—Mason L. Weems was but a mountebank!

He an historian, indeed! Why he laughed over his work,—fiddled even while he wrote—danced during his moments of reflection—never plodded—never could plod,—scratched no bewildered head,—never was at a loss—never hesitated in his progress, but went forward with a promptness and singleness of vision, that never allowed itself to linger at details. If a small fact suited not his great fact, he shoved it aside as unfitted for his purpose. It was enough for him that, satisfied of his hero and his results, he made all things tributary to the glory of the one, and the proper finish of the other.

Besides—greater offence!—he allowed himself to sport with the awful *manes* of the past. He suffered himself to fall into tears and laughter, as the case might be,—and sympathized, like any other human being, in the trials and the triumphs of his favourite. He yielded to the requisitions of humanity, and felt with his subjects— argued the case for them, forgetting that he himself was their judge; and, scorning the accumulation of mere glyphs, preferred a dramatic portraiture which would embody the story at a glance. "How could such a man be a historian!" exclaims the historian, *par excellence*, of our times. Such a man is a picture-fancier, a novelist, a rhapsodist,—what you please—but you must not abuse the dignity of a grave profession, by any misapplication of its title to him. This will never do! . . .

If we deny to Weems the merit of the historian, we cannot deny that he was a man of genius. His books have had a vast circulation, have exercised a wondrous influence over the young minds of the country, have moulded many of our noblest characters. His racy and excellent frankness—his orientalisms, his fluency, the fervency of occasional passages, the spirit of his dialogues,—the cleverness with which he would make his persons swear and swagger, and rebuke them for it,—the pleasing diversity of his pictures,—the great knowledge of life which they represent, and the proper morality which elevated all that he wrote—have united to exercise a greater spell over young America, in past days, than almost any collection of writings within our experience. His style was a possession of his own. . . .

Good sense, an admirable tact, and great shrewdness, lay at the bottom of all he said, and qualified all the extravagances of his speech. He combined, in some degree, the poet and the novelist—the one in the singular smoothness of his rhythm (for his prose is not infrequently passable blank verse); the other, in the happy discrimination of his characters, and the adroitness with which he contrives to put them in opposition and contrast. His rapidity in moments of action is quite Homeric, and the excellent, characteristic speeches, which he puts into the mouths of his personages, would not discredit Plutarch. With all his extravagance, his fondness for colouring, his episodical anecdote (most probably, in half the number of cases, invented for the occasion), his books are yet faithful to all the vital truths of history. . . .

If a small fact suited not his great fact, he shoved it aside as unfitted for his purpose. It was enough for him that, satisfied of his hero and his results, he made all things tributary to the glory of the one, and the proper finish of the other. Besides—greater offense!—he allowed himself to sport over the awful *manes* of the past. He suffered himself to fall into tears and laughter, as the case might be,—and sympathized, like any other human being, in the trials and triumphs of his favourite.

He yielded to the requisitions of humanity, and felt with his subjects—argued the case for them, forgetting that he himself was their judge; and, scorning the accumulation of mere glyphs, preferred a dramatic portraiture which would embody the story at a glance. "How can such a man be a historian!"—exclaims the historian, par *excellence*, of our times. Such a man is a picture fancier, a novelist, a rhapsodist,—what you please—but you must not abuse the dignity if a grave profession, by any misapplication of its title to him. This will never do! . . .

He never appears to have resisted his humour, the direction of which seems always to have been innocent. He yielded himself at once to the situation and the subject, with a degree of *abandon* such as marks the merry witches in the revels of Tam O'Shanter. . . . He could make merry at a wedding with the rest—the music never drove him off—and thus, by giving countenance to what is innocent and natural, he prevented youthful hilarity from rushing to excess. He could visit "tavernes," and very well knew the "tapsteres" thereof, by name, but it was just in such wise as he knew all men, made in the image of God, and worthy, for that reason if for no other, of human consideration and respect;—as he knew the outcast, the profligate, the lowly and the little hoping; as a Priest, properly solicitous of his trusts should know and seek those whom his brethren were but too apt to abandon or avoid.

He had no fear of the vulgar. . . . Nay, we are not sure that there was something of the social aspects of a tavern which . . . may have found favour in his sight. There he met with all the varieties of character, just such motley groups as old Chaucer rode with to Canterbury—men of all fashions and tastes . . . who could teach as well as learn, and, like himself, season the sermon with a story, and the story with a song. . . .

INDEX

Saint Peter's University Library
Withdrawn